BIRDS AT LOUGH BEG

To Walter & Nan
with best wishes
from Gordon

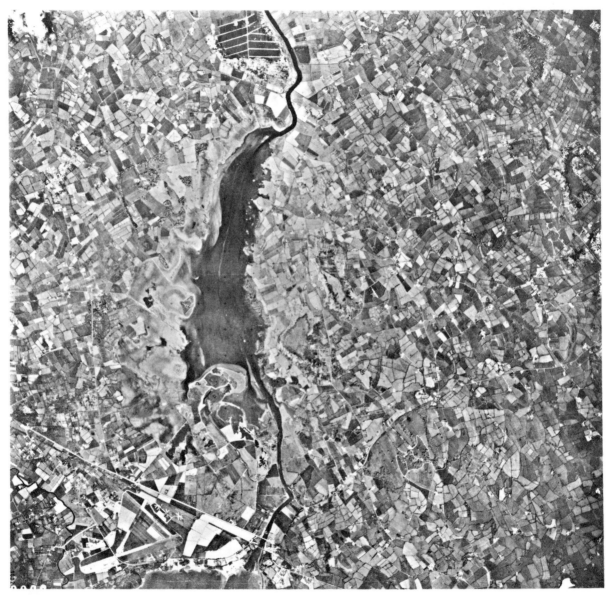

Aerial view of Lough Beg

BIRDS AT LOUGH BEG

GORDON D'ARCY

Blackstaff Press

Published by Blackstaff Press Limited, 255A Upper Newtownards Road, Belfast BT4 3JF.

ISBN 0 85640 120 X

Printed in Northern Ireland by Belfast Litho Printers Limited.

Contents

List of Plates

List of Illustrations

Acknowledgements

I shall not attempt to list all the observers who have watched birds or submitted records from Lough Beg over the years. I'm sure it would amount to hundreds of names and a few might go unacknowledged. Rather, I have reserved my thanks to a few without whose assistance the production of the book would have been impossible.

I am indebted to Mr. T. Ennis for his guidance in many respects of the book; Mr. C. D. Deane for help with the Irish Bird Reports; Mr. N. D. McKee for assistance in compiling the ringing section; Mr. J. Furphy for assistance with the conservation aspect, and to Mr. J. Harron for help with the flora section.

I should like also to thank the Public Records Office of Northern Ireland; the Linen Hall and Central Libraries; the Ulster Museum and the Ordnance Survey of Northern Ireland, all in Belfast.

In the preparation of the introductory chapters, I received much information from local sources. I should like to thank Lady Mulholland, Mr. B. Grant, Mr. J. Doyle, Mr. J. McAteer, and Father Eunan of Portglenone Monastery.

Finally to the advice, encouragement and hard work of Mr. J. Shaw I am especially indebted.

G.D'A.

Rafts of Pochard and Tufted Duck

Lough Beg: The Background

An objective of this book is to bring this small lake to the notice of as many people as possible. I should like to stimulate the interest of other branches of the natural sciences besides ornithology, and to appeal to the non-specialist as well as to the specialist reader.

With the current upsurge of interest in ornithology, many of the best bird-watching areas in Ireland have already been described in publications. It is unfortunate, to my mind, that most of these works have concentrated on southern Ireland. Very good habitats exist in Northern Ireland, and some of them besides Lough Beg (which is perhaps the outstanding ornithological locality in Northern Ireland) would merit documentation.

A paper was produced in 1959 by A. J. Tree on the birds of Lough Beg. It was one of the bulletins of the now defunct Ulster Society for the Protection of Birds. A second was written by J. Donaldson and P. S. Watson in 1963. To both of these papers I am indebted for providing a basis for the systematic list of birds. I feel, however, that Lough Beg now justifies a more comprehensive study.

Besides bird-watching, the Lough Neagh basin is the focus of many interests, including fishing, sailing, water-skiing and wildfowling. While this environment can accomodate some such activities, it is my opinion that those detrimental to wildlife should be restricted. At Newferry, at the northern end of Lough Beg, there is a speedboat/water-ski club which operates in the summer months, causing disturbances to the breeding birds on the lough. Wildfowling has always been a problem and, if not carefully managed, causes wholesale disruption to wintering ducks.

Of late, the north-western shore of the lough has been designated a reserve in which shooting is theoretically banned. I believe that this is inadequate. Lough Beg acts as a bottleneck for the many migrating birds flying through and staying in the Lough Neagh basin. If serious disruption takes place at this 'control valve', the effect on the bird-life of much of Northern Ireland would be serious. For this reason, I should like to see shooting and speedboating prohibited at Lough Beg and the entire area set aside as a nature reserve. If this project was modelled on famous English wildlife reserves, Northern Ireland would have an outstanding conservation area. I do not believe that such measures are out of the question. Lough Neagh is surely large enough to cater for a wide diversity of outdoor interests, including wildfowling and sailing. Indeed, some progress has already been made, for, recently Lough Beg has been recognised as an area of outstanding Scientific Importance and is a consideration of the newly formed Convention of Wetlands.

Only the relative inaccessibility of Lough Beg and its limited industrial potential have so far saved it from development. However, the habitat is being steadily whittled away. Old cars have been dumped, some of the scrub has been cleared, the arable fields have encroached more and more onto the callow lands on the western shore. Some of the excellent areas for birds which were accidentally created by the removal of large quantities of sand at the lough's southern end, have been covered over in the creation of a new farm. However, the open grassy fields, the result of this development, provide good feeding for swans and ducks when winter flooding inundates the meadows.

Environmental change, therefore, has not always proved destructive.

The most serious threat to the wildlife is pollution of the waters of the lake. This could cause the extinction of the very rich sub-aquatic plantlife, so important in the delicate food chain of the fauna. If the source of supply to this chain is adversely affected, not only would the birds which feed on the plants be lost, but this would consequently affect the lower links like insects and fish which rely to an extent on the nutrients generated by the plants. In short, each link is dependent on the others and if the chain is broken, all will suffer. It is therefore of great importance that silage and other toxic effluent is prevented from contaminating the waters of this lough.

The significance of Lough Beg cannot be understated. Should it be set aside as a national reserve, something of its wildlife potential could be realised. Not only would it harbour vast gatherings of wintering birds, but passage migrants could be induced to linger and who can say what rare species might remain to breed in the wild and varied habitat?

HISTORY

Toome is probably so named after the site of an ancient burial mound. It was in fact called 'Fearsat Tuama', the Irish for 'the ford at the tumulus',

Occupying an important crossing place on the Bann, it was well known throughout history and is frequently referred to in the ancient annals of Ireland. Its significance can be, to some extent, inferred from the number and variety of ancient artifacts which have been recovered from the Bann. In the last century, the Board of Works carried out extensive dredging operations, uncovering in the process thousands of flint and stone implements dating from the Stone Age. Many other more recent objects have also been uncovered, including Iron and Bronze Age shields, spears and swords.

In the twelfth century AD, the followers of De Courcy built a castle at Toome which has unfortunately long since disappeared, its stones having been used in the construction of the 18th century bridge across the Bann.

Church Island, on the west shore of Lough Beg, has a remarkable history of its own. It is the site of an ancient monastic settlement dating from long before the Norman Invasion. The Irish name of the island and its parish was Inis Toide and is mentioned in the Annals of Inis Fallen in 1112 and in the Annals of Ulster in 1129.

The Vikings, who sailed up the Bann from the sea in their long boats, stopped at Church Island to ravage the settlement, which nevertheless survived such attacks and was eventually reorganised in the time of Malachy, Bishop of Armagh.

The lands on both sides of the lough belonged to the monastery in early times. Later, the clan Ó Scolláin became the 'erenagh' or guardian of the area — hence the name Ballyscullion.

On the first Sunday in September 1910, the ancient pilgrimage to Church Island was revived and has been continued annually ever since. Up until comparatively recent times, burials were still being carried out there, the funeral cortege having to wade through the floodwaters on at least one occasion to carry out their task. The island also boasts an ancient well (a large boulder with a cup-shaped depression therein) whose waters were believed to have had healing properties. Pilgrims to the well tied rags to an overhanging tree by way of symbolic offerings for alleged cures. Sadly, this custom, part of Lough Beg's rich folklore, has more or less fallen into disuse. On a happier note, a fair which was traditionally held in Toome and had gradually slipped into oblivion a few decades ago, has been revived by some of the townspeople.

The illustrious Earl Bishop of Derry was responsible for the erection of a spire on the old church of Church

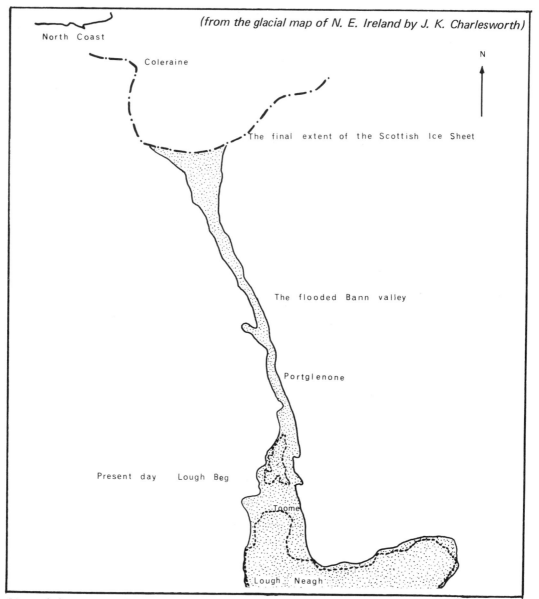

(from the glacial map of N. E. Ireland by J. K. Charlesworth)

North Coast

Coleraine

N

The final extent of the Scottish Ice Sheet

The flooded Bann valley

Portglenone

Present day   Lough Beg

Toome

Lough Neagh

Map of the Bann Valley in Post Glacial times

Megaceros giganteus: the Giant Irish Deer

Island in the 18th century. His motive in building this 'folly' was to add an ecclesiastic note which would enhance the scenery. Ironically, an RAF Blenheim aircraft crashed on the island during the 1939-45 war killing the crew.

GEOLOGY

The geological history of the Lough Neagh basin probably began in the Tertiary era, with a localised collapse of the upper strata at the western edge of the basalt plateau which now mantles County Antrim. There is evidence that a lake existed in this depression before the Ice Age, but it was not until the final retreat of the ice sheet that Lough Neagh, as we know it today, was formed. On the last retreat, some ten thousand years ago, vast quantities of melt-water inundated the area, forming post-glacial Lake Neagh.[1] This lake, considerably more extensive than at present, extended to the north-west in a long narrow sheet of water. It was probably stemmed off a few miles from the north coast by the terminal moraine due to the final advance of the ice. A rise in sea level, due to the melting of the glaciers, further ponded back a northern drainage path till only a few thousand years ago.

By the time the Lower Bann river system became stabilised, Lough Beg remained as a shallow enlargement of the river, a short distance from the north western corner of the larger lake. Evidence of the glaciation is widespread. Drumlins exist on both sides of Lough Beg, though those near the water are generally low and obscure. The small islands on the western side are probably drumlins surrounded by thick alluvial deposits. The existence of large boulders on top of these deposits are difficult to explain outside a glacial context. At the southern end of the Lough, the fluvio-glacial sands have been commercially worked in the past. In these outwash deposits, the skull and antlers of *Megaceros giganteus*, the giant Irish deer, have been found.

In the warm climate of the immediate post-glacial era, vegetation flourished, forming a layer of peat over the alluvial plain surrounding Lough Beg. This is overlain by a layer of diatomite or Kieselguhr, a fossil soil formed by the silicaceous remains of millions of diatoms — warm climate algae. Electrical insulation and cosmetic powder are among the by-products of this material, and it is still worked in the Creagh.[2]

The discovery of hand-worked rock and the remains of a dugout, within the diatomaceous clay, indicate

1. *The Geology of Ireland*, J K Charlesworth
2. *A Regional Geology of Northern Ireland*, The Geological Survey of Northern Ireland

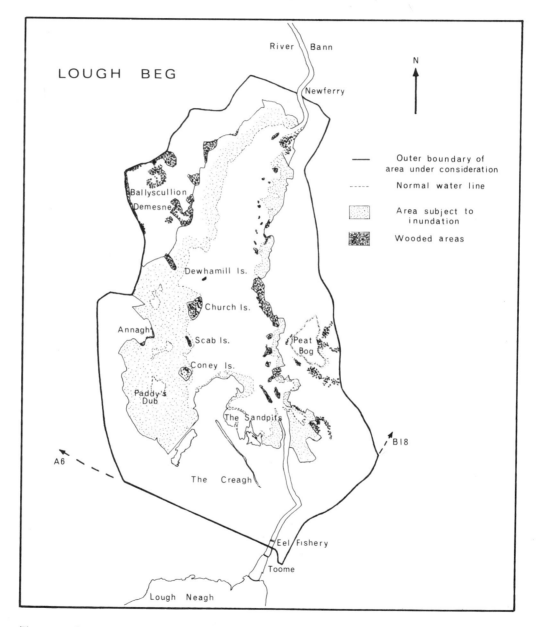

Topographical map of Lough Beg

that man inhabited the area of Toome some eight thousand years ago. This makes Toome one of man's earliest settlements in Ireland.

TOPOGRAPHY

The scale drawing on page 5 shows the location of the features referred to in this section.

The Lough lies about one and a half miles north of Toome on the River Bann. It is approximately three miles from north to south, and about a mile at its widest. Although it is generally shallow, a deeper navigation channel runs along its length. This can be clearly seen in the aerial photograph.

Up until the 1930s, the surface area was much greater than it is today. Flood gates were constructed at the exit of the Lower Bann from Lough Neagh. As a result, a low water level has been maintained during the summer at Lough Beg. Extensive grassy meadows have developed naturally on the western side of the lake. In summers of low precipitation, mudflats are often exposed in the bays between the small islands on this side. These meadows become partially or totally flooded in the winter.

The sand deposits at the southern end were commercially exploited earlier this century. Long since abandoned, a varied terrain of lagoons, islands and sandpits remains, which is overgrown with brambles, gorse and other low vegetation.

Much of the eastern shore is covered with alder and willow, and is fringed with a few sizeable reed beds. There are also a number of freshwater lagoons and islets. A raised bog is to be found well back from the water's edge about half way along this shore, and another exists at the northern end. Another feature of the area is the mixed woodlands of the Ballyscullion Estate, which contains the largest deciduous trees at the Lough. About ten streams flow into the lake, some of which form shallow, marshy ponds near the Lough proper.

In days gone by, two sections of the Bann flowed into the southern end. The section which ran through the Creagh has silted up, and is now overgrown with weeds and reeds. Many interesting aquatic plants are found in this now stagnant waterway.

The normal summer surface area of the lake is around 1,300 acres, but winter flooding of the low-lying callow land may increase this surface area by as much as 100%.

FLORA AND NON-AVIAN FAUNA

It is outside the scope of this book to detail the vast array of the organisms of Lough Beg. It should, however, be brought to the reader's notice that the area is very rich in all sorts of wildlife besides the avifauna.

An idea of the significance of the flora of the area can be imagined from the following extract from the proceedings of the Belfast Naturalists' Field Club, which records an excursion to Lough Beg on a June day at the turn of the century.

'This district is well known in botanical circles as yielding many plants of exceeding variety, and on this occasion, several of these species were found. Here is the only station in Great Britain for the hoary sedge (*Carex buxbaumii*), and even here it occupies only a few square yards. It is almost a pity that it should be so scarce, it being, perhaps, the most elegant of our sedges. Those who dread the extinction of our rare native plants need not be apprehensive on account of the visit of the Belfast Field Club to Toome — only two specimens of this rarity were brought away as souvenirs of an interesting excursion. Many other species of carex were observed in full flower, including the sedge (*Carex curta*), and the tufted sedge (*Carex stricta*).

'The northern bed-straw (*Galium boreale*) was found just coming into flower, and also the spindle tree (*Euonymus europaeus*), which was once prized on account of the toughness of its wood. The purple sandwort (*Lepigonum rubrum*) was gathered on the shores of Lough Beg. Only two other stations have been previously recorded for this plant in Ireland; growing along with the sandwort was *Leontodon taraxicum var palustre*, a scarce form. A search over the extensive peat bog close to Toome brought to view the tiny, thread-like stems and elegant, crimson flowers of the cranberry (*Vaccinium oxycoccus*) here occurring in abundance, and here also is found the crowberry (*Empetrum nigrum*), called in the vernacular of the district "mannox heather". The berries of this species, which only ripen in Autumn, were found to be in some cases already well formed. In the moors of North Britain, where the crowberry is produced in profusion, its fruit affords a coveted food for the grouse and ptarmigan, as well as for the bird whose name it bears.

'...Many plants of less note were obtained, and had the season been further advanced, several other botanical rarities might have been collected.'

FLORA

The flora of Lough Beg, as it exists today, cannot be satisfactorily discussed without first considering the different habitats at the lake. Consequently, the area shown on the topographic map may be subdivided into a few distinct zones of widely differing plant types:

(a) The meadows of the western shore.
    This area is, generally, of little botanical interest and comprises mainly grasses and rushes. It is considered that flooding and constant grazing prevents more growth, such as alder and willow, from getting a foothold.

(b) The Sandpits and Creagh to the south.
    Old maps of Lough Beg indicate that this area was at one time overgrown with scrub. The abandonment of the more recent sandworkings has given rise to a new type of rough scrubland comprising broom, whin, thorn, crab apple etc. Agricultural reclamation in the past few years has destroyed much of this growth.

(c) The Ballyscullion Demesne on the western side. This is woodland area planted largely in the eighteenth century. The trees are mainly deciduous though with a few groups of Scots pines at the northern end. The main types are ash, beech, sycamore, elm, hairy and silver birch, and a few oak, blackthorn and elder.

(d) The eastern fringe of the lake is covered in alder, willow and the occasional hazel. The spindle tree and guelder rose grow in a few places. Extensive reed beds are to be found in the bays along this shore. A large variety of woodland plants grow along this shore amongst the trees.

(e) The Lough proper has a very rich plant life existing as emergent aquatic and sub-aquatic varieties. The inflowing streams and disused waterways are rich in flora and in some places are so undisturbed as to have good representative populations of the plant life of a century ago which has been destroyed in other places.

(f) Some uncut peat still exists at the eastern edge of the area which contains a few unusual plants.

The plant types fall into the following broad groupings:

SUB-AQUATICS: These are the plants which grow beneath the surface of the water with their roots in the bottom. They comprise mainly waterwort, bladderwort, water crowfoot, water milfoil. (*Elatine hydropiper*), a subspecies of waterwort and water starwort, both scarce in Northern Ireland, are widespread at Lough Beg.

AQUATICS:
(a) Algae do not grow in profusion at Lough Beg due to the relatively unpolluted condition of the water at present. The bacteria which is responsible for the disruption of the natural plant life of many parts of Lough Neagh does not appear to contaminate Lough Beg: possibly due to the obstruction at the flood gates at Toome.
(b) In the still water regions, a little removed from the Lough proper, a few species of floating plants survive, including yellow water lily and arrowhead.

EMERGENT PLANTS: In the comparatively still water areas, including the quieter bays on the shores of the lake, these plant types prosper. The commonest are reed mace, common reed, dwarf spike-rush, reedgrass and bullrush (sparse). Sedges of the varieties bottle sedge and bladder sedge are most widespread. Rare sedges (*segosia*) and (*hudsoni*) are also found. A rare grass, northern small reed, is to be found in one or two localities on both shores.

The grasses and reeds are often accompanied by yellow or purple loosestrife, or woody nightshade.

In slow-moving water flowering rush, horsetails and bur-reed are found.

WOODLAND FLORA: A variety of fern-life covers many areas in the woods. Interesting flowers of a great diversity are found in this habitat, including wood speedwell, wood anemone, wild garlic, stitchwort, gipsywort and ragged robin.

One family of plants warrants special attention: the orchids. Three species are found, two of which are rarities. The common marsh orchid is represented by both purple and spotted varieties. Irish Ladies' Tresses Orchid is found in one or two localities in most years and the beautiful Butterfly Orchid has been found at the lough on more than one occasion.

FAUNA
Eels, bream, perch and pike comprise the commonest coarse fish, whilst salmon and dolloghan occur in season. The long-standing eel fishery at Toome is a testimony to the traffic of this species through Lough Beg.

Many species of freshwater molluscs have been found in the waters of the lake, including the bubble snail and the ammonite-like coil snail. The population density of freshwater crustacea, especially the tiny shrimp (*Gammarus tigrinus*), is extremely high.

Of the larger mammals, badgers, foxes, rabbits and hares abound, and stoats have been seen but are more localised. Otters are well known, both along the Bann and in Lough Beg itself. Rats, mice and bats are amongst the smaller mammals represented.

As an area full of wildlife of all kinds, its significance can hardly be emphasised enough. It would provide an excellent all-round natural history study for an enthusiast. I am concerned here specifically with the birds, but I should hope that while the habitat remains in its relatively unspoilt form, a study of the other living things will at some stage be undertaken by another author.

THE BIRD SPECIES
A total of 171 species has been identified at Lough Beg up to the end of 1976. These can conveniently be categorized into:

(a) RESIDENTS: birds which may be found at the Lough throughout the year. About sixty species fall into this grouping, a few of which are non-breeders.
(b) SUMMER VISITORS: birds which migrate to the Lough in the summer to breed. About twenty species come to the Lough to breed from more southerly wintering grounds.
(c) PASSAGE MIGRANTS: birds which migrate

through the Lough en route to summer or winter grounds. About sixty species are migrants in spring and autumn.

(d) WINTER VISITORS: birds which come to the Lough during the winter. About thirty species are winter visitors.

(e) VAGRANTS: birds which have been recorded less than five times. About forty species are vagrants to the area.

There is considerable overlapping from one group to the next, ie some species are both passage migrants and winter visitors. For example the Lapwing is a resident but is also a passage migrant and a winter visitor in large numbers. The Meadow Pipit not only nests widely in the area but is also a passage migrant and the resident population is swollen by individuals from outside the area during the winter.

The species total may not seem high in comparison with other bird-watching stations around Ireland. Cape Clear, Co Cork, for example, has an impressive total of nearly 250 species. It should be kept in mind, however, that an isolated coastal island is a much more attractive proposition to migrating passerines than is an inland lake. As far as wildfowl and waders are concerned, Lough Beg is of unique significance.

The sheer volume of birds inhabiting the area is outstanding for an inland lake. On a day in winter there may be ten thousand ducks on the 2,500 acre lake. This waterfowl density is virtually unequalled in the whole of Ireland.

Due to the lacustrine nature of the area, it goes without saying that the majority of the bird species to be seen at Lough Beg may be classified loosely as 'water birds'. Indeed, sixty percent of the recorded birds have an association with water as their natural environment. Prominent amongst them are the waterfowl and waders, and these are, naturally enough, discussed in detail in the text.

It remains to deal with the other forty per cent of Lough Beg's bird species. Although the habitat is varied and there is an abundant passerine population, there is a limited diversity of species in this category. The largest group, finches, has about a dozen representatives. Next largest, the thrushes, has about ten. Warblers, crows, and tits have six or less species each represented at Lough Beg.

One group which warrants a mention is the birds of prey. Ten have been recorded, including goshawk, osprey, and three species of owl. With the diversity of wildlife in the area it is understandably a good place for birds of prey. Kestrels, sparrow hawks and merlins can be regularly seen hunting in the varied habitat and the occasional hen harrier may be seen on passage quartering the water meadows.

There is evidence that certain passerine species use the Bann as a flightline on passage migration. There is a regular build-up of swifts, hirundines and warblers in the autumn. In recent years a seasonal movement of wheatears, pipits, wagtails and larks has come to light. The redstart seen some years ago may have been a migrant, or may have bred in the area. Unfortunately, the smaller, more elusive, passerines are somewhat ignored by observers visiting the area, who tend to concentrate on the more obvious, the waterfowl and waders. Much might yet be discovered about resident and migrant passeriforms, especially in the ideal woodland habitat along the Antrim shore of the Lough.

Some reference should be made to a few species of birds which seem to have disappeared from the area due, at least in part, to human interference. The yellow wagtail bred in the Lough Neagh basin in gradually decreasing numbers until 1942. The last of the original colony nested at Lough Beg in that year and it has not been proved to have bred there since. Watson and Donaldson regarded the partridge as a scarce resident but it may well have vanished also.

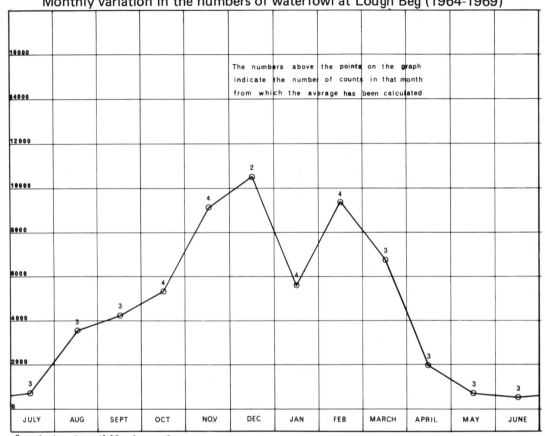

Monthly variation in the numbers of waterfowl at Lough Beg (1964-1969)

The numbers above the points on the graph indicate the number of counts in that month from which the average has been calculated

Graph of variation in wildfowl numbers

FEATURES TO BE NOTED ON GRAPH

(a)   Low numbers of waterfowl in the summer months; mostly breeding mallard, shelduck, tufted duck.

(b)   Sudden rise in August, due mainly to post-breeding accumulation of mallard.

(c)   Steady rise until the end of October. Passage coots, teal, shoveler, pintail, wigeon.

(d)   Sudden rise at the end of October, November, December. Mass arrival of diving ducks.

(e)   The acute tooth in the graph in January is due mainly to the exodus of waterfowl. There are probably two contributory factors (1) Shooting intensity (2) Natural commutation between Loughs Beg and Neagh.

(f)   Steady decline in the period late February-March. Wintering and passage wildfowl move out.

(g)   Less acute decline, April-mid-May. Lingering passage teal, shoveler, pintail.

Pintail, corncrake, nightjar, dunlin, oystercatcher and common sandpiper have only the most slender claim as breeding birds in the area.

Since June 1963 a new species has taken up residence — the collared dove — and has become abundant in the farms in the area. It is an unfortunate fact, though, that those species lost to the Lough are unlikely to be compensated for by new arrivals.

WATERFOWL

A paper entitled 'Winter and Passage Wildfowl at Lough Beg' was compiled in 1966 by J Donaldson. This is a resumé of wildfowl counts from as early as 1953, including regular monthly winter wildfowl counts begun in late 1963. The Northern Ireland Ornithologists' Club carried out an intensive programme of monthly counts for the complete Lough Neagh basin in the latter half of the 1960s. Lough Beg's wildfowl was counted thirty-eight times by the NIOC between January 1965 and January 1969. In addition, I have many personal counts over the past fifteen years to augment the accumulation of data already in existence. It is for another author to discuss the findings of the wildfowl counts in the Lough Neagh basin as a whole. I am here concerned only with the waterfowl at Lough Beg.

As a result of the NIOC counts, numerous statistics relating to the twenty odd species of waterfowl considered have been compiled. I have, however, included a minimum of tabular information, to avoid overburdening the reader with an excess of statistical data. The graph (above) shows the seasonal variation of the waterfowl at the Lough. Peak figures are well over 10,000 and may be as high as 15,000 in winter. They fall to a few hundred in mid-summer — an indication of the large numbers of waterfowl using the lake as a wintering resort. There is obvious consistency in the counts over the period March to August, for the four year period. During the shooting season, however, from 1 September to 28 February, the counts vary considerably — an indication of the considerable disturbance experienced by the wildfowl of the lake. The graph indicates averages over the four year period. Some of the counts were, however, well in excess of the peak figure shown, and one February count was as high as 15,500.

Surface feeding ducks are a feature of Lough Beg. The average wintering totals are about a third of the total wintering in the whole Lough Neagh basin, whilst the March and April figures are generally 50%-60% of the total.

Usually about 10% of the wintering diving ducks of the basin are to be found at Lough Beg.

WILDFOWLING:

The sporting rights of the lake have been leased to the major gun clubs and syndicates. There are several represented, the major ones being the Bann Valley Gun Club and the South Derry Gun Club, both of which operate on the western shore. Their designated areas are, respectively, the north-western sector and the south-western sector. With the other clubs and syndicates, the total number of guns licensed to shoot at Lough Beg is in the hundreds. Although only a fraction of these wildfowlers regularly shoot at the Lough, many turn out at the start of the winter shooting season.

The situation at present is, from the conservationist's point of view, more acceptable than was the case in the past. There was previously a 'free for all' in which many protected birds were shot as well as the traditional targets — the surface feeding ducks.

Since the Bann Valley Gun Club acquired the rights to the north-western sector, a refuge has been established in which shooting is very infrequent. This measure has done a good deal towards the conservation of the wintering waterfowl at Lough Beg. In fact, there appears to have been an increase in the

Migrating Whimbrel over Church Island

number of surface-feeding ducks, especially wigeon, in the past decade.

Credit is due to the gun clubs at Lough Beg not only for their progressive approach to wildfowling and its management, but also for their co-operation with other bodies in WAGBI* schemes.

MIGRATION

The Lower Bann lies generally in a north/south linea-tion, with an extensive estuarine mouth near Castle-

rock, and at the southern end, the largest freshwater lake in the British Isles, Lough Neagh. Between Castlerock and Lough Neagh, there are virtually no 'stop off' areas for migrating birds until Lough Beg is reached. That the river is used as a flyway by many species of birds is beyond question.

The monks at Portglenone Monastery are well aware of the movements of birds, especially waterfowl, along the Bann, to the north of Lough Beg. Flocks of wild swans and cormorants are most common. However, both surface-feeding and diving ducks have been seen flying along the line of the river, mostly in the latter

*WAGBI Wildfowlers' Association of Great Britain and Ireland

part of the year. The characteristic whistling of the goldeneye in flight has been heard after dark.

Wild geese have been seen at Portglenone on a number of occasions, including once a skein of over 100. As a rule, the geese have not followed the river valley but have appeared from the north-west and flown off to the east.

In the spring and autumn, good numbers of ducks, waders and gulls are to be found at the Bann mouth. Rarities have turned up there on many occasions, and some of the more unusual species, like garganey, black tern, little gull and the uncommon sandpipers appear at Lough Beg and Castlerock in the same seasons, indicating the link between the two areas. Similarly, the south shore of Lough Neagh, especially the Reedy Flat area, is an accumulation spot for migrants, which suggests the possibility of a southern passage through the midlands of Ireland.

Migration through Lough Beg also occurs to and from the northwest and the east. In recent years, arrivals and departures of northern species (wild swans, golden plovers) have been observed from and towards the Sperrin mountains to the northwest. These birds probably accumulate at the south shore of Lough Foyle, fly directly to Lough Beg from there, and return to Lough Foyle before departure to their northern breeding grounds. Great-crested grebes and shelducks perform a local migratory movement to the sea after the breeding season. Both are found in hundreds in Belfast Lough in the late autumn and winter. It is likely that the populations of each, in the Lough Neagh basin, move eastwards to the estuarine loughs in the latter half of the year, and return again in the spring. Very few of either species are to be found on the lakes in winter.

In addition to the above movements, Lough Beg acts as an accumulation point for some bird species in spring and autumn. Prominent amongst the autumnal species are locally bred swallows, swifts and warblers. Those of the spring are mainly golden plovers, lapwings, northern thrushes and larks.

Passage migrants have been observed, though more frequently heard at night over Toome. Among those which have been identified by call, during the night, are whimbrel, curlew, wigeon, goldeneye, wild swans, redwings and fieldfares.

Local movements of wildfowl take place between Lough Neagh and Lough Beg throughout the winter months. This is due largely to disturbance from shooting, and feeding movements, rather than normal return passage.

Certain waders have been observed flying straight through the Lough or stopping only briefly. Examples are sanderling, green sandpiper, whimbrel, knot and turnstone. It is highly probable that many others go through unnoticed, only a percentage staying behind long enough to be observed. The actual volume, as distinct from the observed volume of migrating birds, is consequently the object of considerable speculation. It has come to the notice of some observers that at peak migration times the passage bird population of the lough may change dramatically in the course of a single day. It is possible to cover the lough, noting the numbers of the species present, and on the return trip, covering the same ground, to encounter quite different numbers. This is especially true in the autumn, and the birds most concerned seem to be waders. To my mind, this implies that migration of many of the birds is at times constant, and very often occurs at an altitude higher than normal vision. It is mainly when the flocks are influenced by factors like adverse weather conditions, the need for feeding or rest, that they tend to 'stop off' at Lough Beg.

There is nevertheless an uncanny regularity in the pattern of migration at the lough, it being possible to predict the arrival times of many species.

Autumnal passage is for most species heavier than that of spring. From August to November, large

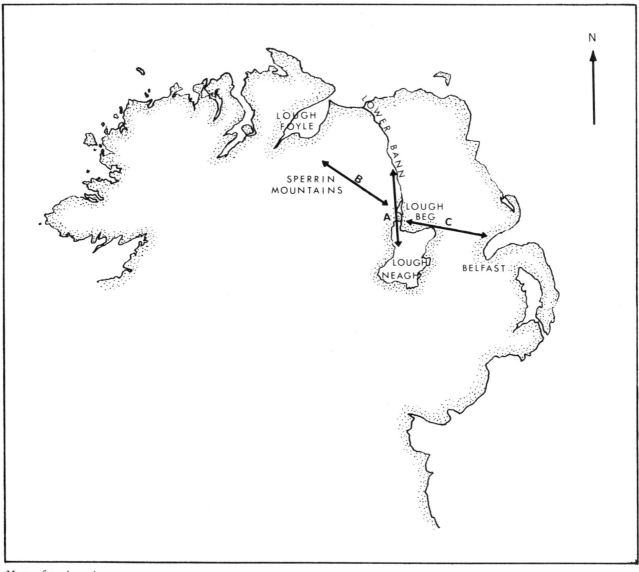

Map of main migratory routes
A The Lower Bann flyway
B The Northwestern connection
C The Eastern connection

numbers of waterfowl and waders move generally southwards through the lough. Wild swans, surface feeding ducks, coots, small numbers of geese, are amongst the waterfowl passing through in the months of October and November. The transit of waders occurs earlier, reaching peak numbers in September. Plovers, shanks, ruffs, godwits, stints and a variety of sandpipers comprise this passage. Accompanying species are terns, gulls, birds of prey and a few smaller passerine species. Rare and uncommon wading birds tend to occur at this time.

The spring, on the other hand, has certain typical migrants like whimbrel, black-tailed godwits and ringed plover, and, more rarely, little gull and spotted redshank. Characteristic ducks of the spring at the lake are pintail, shoveler, goldeneye, gadwall and the occasional garganey.

Arrivals of warblers, hirundines, cuckoos and swifts may be observed in the early summer and the copses and farm buildings support fair breeding populations of these summer visitors.

Weather conditions are important in bird migration. At Lough Beg, during peak migration times, the prevailing winds have a significant influence on the species which occur at the lake. This often constitutes the difference between a poor and a good year for some migrants, especially certain waders, terns and gulls. A steady easterly air flow in spring and autumn can mean the occurrence of good numbers of shanks, stints, sandpipers, black terns etc. Southerly winds tend to accentuate the westerly drift of many of these continental migrants. American species are more likely to turn up after strong westerly winds. This is particularly the case if these have originated in the Gulf of Mexico as hurricanes and have remained intact enough on reaching the Irish coastline.

The branch of ornithology known as migration is far from being completely understood. It is full of bewildering contradictions and mysteries, and has been the subject of many volumes. There exist many good stations around Ireland which are used to observe migrating birds, but few are inland lakes. Just as much information has already been accumulated about Lough Beg's migrants, there is much to learn and even more, perhaps, that will never be known.

In 1976 the author visited the lough on some fifty occasions, mainly in an effort to enlarge upon the information regarding migration. Some interesting observations were made, which substantiate many of the deductions drawn in the early part of this chapter. The observations are below in chronological order.

7.4.76 A large accumulation (c1500) golden plover were on the meadows near the Annagh. Parties of about twenty were observed flying out of the flock, climbing high in the sky, and flying steadily off to the N.W. (direction of the Sperrins).

18.4.76 The accumulation had grown to 2,500 (considerably larger than the wintering flock). They were constantly gathering for departure. By the end of the month only forty were still in the area.

18.4.76 Three little stints were watched flying out of Paddy's Dub and flying high directly out of the lough.

23.4.76 A flock of ninety-three whimbrel gathered in small groups at Coney Island towards dusk. All arrivals were from the south. (Probably a migratory roost.)

13.5.76 A compact flock of seventy knots flew into the lough from the south, across the Creagh. They flew down from a height, looked as though they might land, but instead flew on north out of the lough along the line of the Lower Bann.

This species is quite rare at the lough in spring. There were many migrants in the area on the same day.

12.8.76 Some 3,000 swallows gathered towards evening and proceeded southwards in waves of one

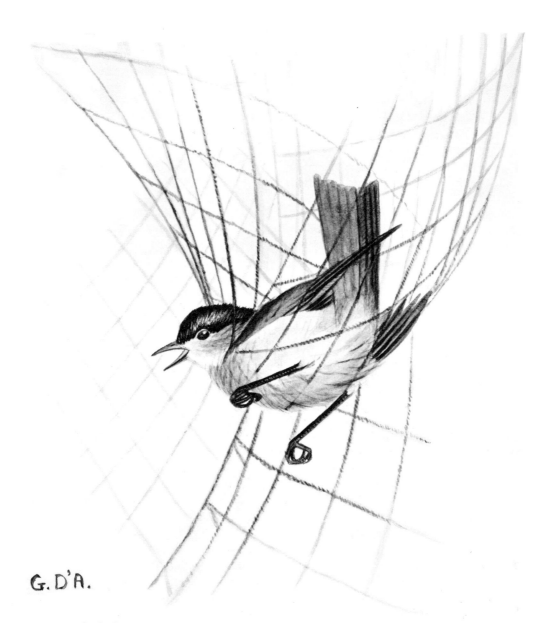

G. D'A.

Mist-netted Blackcap

16

hundred or so at a time. It is probable that these hirundines were going to roost outside the area rather than moving off on migration. (Similar activity noted throughout the month).

30.8.76 A flock of waders flew into the lough from the south, dropping down from altitude at Coney Island. They comprised eight spotted redshanks and five golden plover — they did not stop at the lough but flew out to the north.

10.9.76 Thirteen shelducks flew into the lough from the north, proceeded south and flew out of the area towards Lough Neagh.

Two flocks comprising eighty cormorants flew north over the lough along the line of the Bann at an altitude of over 1,000 feet. (Commutation between Lough Neagh and the north coast.)

23.9.76 An obvious 'fall' of pied wagtails; over 100 on the western meadows including one flock of fifty.

A constant south-easterly wind had been blowing previous to observation.

28.9.76 A black tern was watched flying south along the western shore and off towards Lough Neagh, without stopping .

A flock of eleven pink-footed geese flew into the lough from altitude. They settled for a short while and then flew out of the area directly eastwards.

29.10.76 A party of eight grey-lag and two white-fronted geese flew in from the west, settled on the water amongst wild swans for a while, then flew off to the south on being disturbed.

15.11.76 A flock of fifteen grey-lag geese flew in from the north west and flew off directly to the east without stopping.

A flock of about 100 wigeon were observed flying in and joining over 2,500 others massed at the northern end of the lough.

A party of six goldeneye were seen flying south, out of Lough Beg towards Lough Neagh — altitude about 300 feet.

The above are selected observations noted in the course of a single year. They are, however, indicative of the larger scale activity. Migration 'as it happens' can be observed at Lough Beg. The observation of waterfowl and waders actually engaged on their seasonal movements is a phenomenon which is restricted to few localities in Britain.

RARITIES

It is customary to regard species which have occurred less than ten times in an area as vagrants. However, Lough Beg is a small area and a substantial percentage of the species seen there have occurred on only a few occasions. It is thus convenient to regard those species seen there less than five times as vagrants. About a quarter of the total list falls into this category.

Prominent amongst the vagrants are twelve pelagic or coastal species. Occasionally, such wanderers turn up dead or in an emaciated state after storms.

Eight of the vagrants are of American origin. They generally appear at migration times, in spring, or more often, in autumn. It is thought that they arrive in Ireland after having flown the Atlantic involuntarily, during westerly gales. Two other North American species, pectoral and buff-breasted sandpiper, are almost regular autumnal visitors. The regularity of their appearance gives rise to speculation on the extent of their arctic breeding grounds and the possibility of a regional shift in their age-old migration routes.

A further eight vagrants originated in central or eastern Europe or Eurasia, and turned up at Lough Beg, well removed from their normal range.

Understandably, many of the vagrants have occurred in the spring or autumn, and observation is intensified during these periods. However, stragglers like stork, broad-billed sandpiper and others are unpredictable and could turn up at almost any time during the year.

Finally, a couple of species have occurred at Lough Beg, which, due to circumstantial evidence or for other reasons, cannot be regarded as genuine wanderers. These are listed in the Appendix.

RINGING

Over the past twenty years, small scale ringing has been carried out on the birds of the Lough Beg area. In recent years, however, due to the poor recovery rate, the activity has lessened considerably.

In 1958, 600 young black-headed gulls were ringed on one of the lake's islands, as were eighteen young common terns. Recoveries of the gulls were mainly from the Northern Irish coastline. No tern recoveries have come to light as yet.

Mist netting was used to trap birds in summer 1963, with a fair degree of success. A total of 233 birds were ringed, of twenty-seven species. The list is tabulated:-

RINGING (Tabulation)

4 snipe	13 robin
2 curlew	1 grasshopper warbler
1 common sandpiper	3 sedge warbler
8 dunnock	2 whitethroat
21 black-headed gull	33 willow warbler
45 swallow	4 chiffchaff
26 sandmartin	1 goldcrest
5 great tit	2 greenfinch
15 blue tit	2 linnet
3 coal tit	11 chaffinch
4 wren	2 reed bunting
2 mistle thrush	9 house sparrow
3 song thrush	3 blackbird
8 hedge sparrow	

This method has been used fairly regularly since 1963 and many more birds have been trapped and ringed. A few other species have been added to the above list, including many long-tailed tits and redpolls. Indeed, were it not for the trapping of a few blackcaps in the past decade, the species would be virtually unknown to the area.

Recoveries have been few, and it is impossible at this stage to build up a picture of passerine movement through the area, based on ringing results.

As earlier mentioned, the smaller, more elusive, species tend to be ignored in preference for the more obvious water birds. An intense programme of mist netting at the peak migration periods could provide much additional information about the more secretive passeriformes.

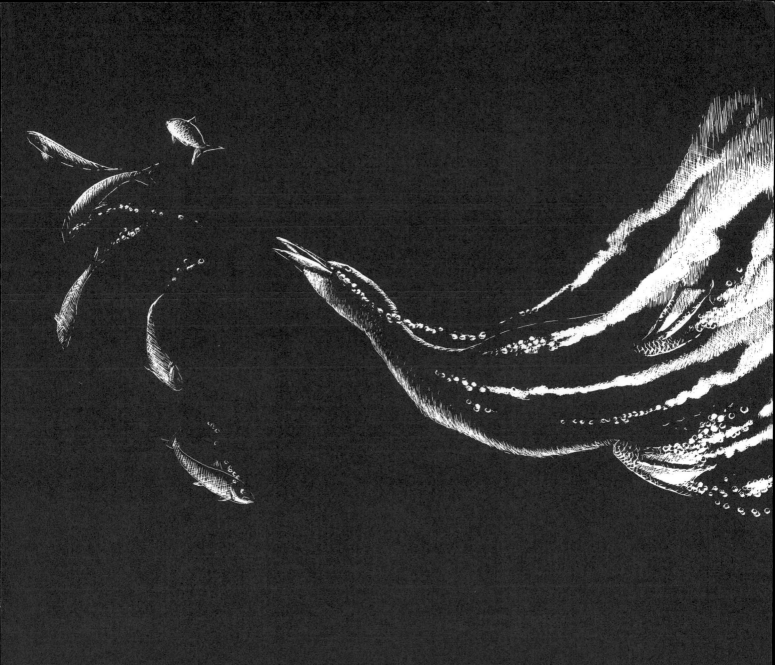

Great Northern Diver

Gordon D'Arcy

19

Little Egret

Gordon D'Arcy

Spoonbill

Gordon D'Arcy

21

A pair of Pintail

Gordon D'Arcy

The Birds at Lough Beg

GREAT NORTHERN DIVER (*Gavia immer*); vagrant
  inland
A single record: one in summer plumage was shot in
River Bann, at Toome, in the winter of 1951/52. It
was examined in the hand at the time.

RED-THROATED DIVER (*Gavia stellata*); vagrant
  inland
A single record: one was found dead on the west shore
on 7 March 1963. There are several records of divers
for Lough Neagh, in the winter.

GREAT-CRESTED GREBE (*Podiceps cristatus*);
  summer resident
A small number breed, usually not more than about
twelve pairs, but in 1963 about twenty pairs nested.
At present it breeds at the sandpits, at a couple of
localities on the east shore, and on one or two of the
islets, notably Dewhamill.

By the autumn, most of the grebes have left the
lough. It is possible that they go to make up part of
the post-breeding flock of up to 750, which is to be
found on Belfast Lough in the autumn.

It is unusual to find more than twenty on any day
during the winter.

An unusually high concentration was sixty-three
adult birds on 31 August, 1958.

LITTLE GREBE (*Tachybaptus ruficollis*); uncommon
  visitor
It has appeared mainly in autumn or winter. Recent
sightings have been in August, September, October
and December. A maximum of thirteen was seen on
22 December, 1963.

It has been noticed a few times in the quiet bays on
the eastern shore of the lake.

On 26 September 1976, an adult was observed
feeding a juvenile in a pond at the sandpits. As the
juvenile appeared to be several months old, it is
probable that it had been reared outside the area of
the lough and had wandered to the sandpits with its
parent.

FULMAR (*Fulmarus glacialis*); vagrant inland
One record: a single bird was observed on the lough
on 20 August 1967.

LEACH'S PETREL (*Oceanodroma leucorrhoa*); vagrant
  inland
One record: one was found dead at Toome in October,
1952.

This pelagic species occasionally experiences 'wrecks'
which carry stragglers far inland. In the 'wreck' of
1952, Leach's petrels were encountered in many parts
of Northern Ireland.

GANNET (*Sula bassana*); vagrant inland
Three records: an immature on 22 October 1960,
another seen autumn 1972 (exact date unknown) and
one found dead, October 1976.

The birds which appear at the lough are probably
strays from one of the North Atlantic breeding
stations. It is notable that they were all sub-adult, and
turned up after the breeding season.

CORMORANT (*Phalacrocorax carbo*); common visitor
Small groups of this species commute between the Bann mouth at Castlerock and Lough Neagh. Skeins comprising up to seventy-five birds together may be seen flying high over Lough Beg. The numbers to be seen on the Lough proper have diminished. Formerly found in numbers of up to sixty, it is unusual nowadays to see more than twenty in a day.

On 5 April, 1964, two grey-headed cormorants were seen on the lough. These may have been of the southern race, but identification due to this feature is not now regarded as conclusive.

SHAG (*Phalacrocorax aristotelis*); vagrant inland
One record: one seen with cormorants on 19 August 1963.

Although they consort with cormorants at the Bann mouth, shags prefer a rocky coastline. It is most unusual for the species to venture inland with the cormorants.

HERON (*Ardea cinera*); resident
At present, this species breeds in two of the woods on the north-west border of the lough, and it may also nest at the south-east.

The breeding population fluctuates, but up to twenty-eight nests have been found. After the severe winter of 1962/63, only fourteen pairs were noted. In 1964, however, seventeen pairs nested and the increase appears to have continued since then. The 1976 colony comprised twenty-three nests.

Heron numbers build up in February, some appearing at the nests towards the end of that month. The colony is not fully occupied until March, and good numbers of herons may be seen about the lough in April and May.

A few are to be found throughout the winter around the lake.

LITTLE EGRET (*Egretta garzetta*); vagrant
The first record was of a single bird on 5 June 1976. One, perhaps the same bird, was seen on several dates in August of the same year.

WHITE STORK (*Ciconia ciconia*); vagrant
A single record: one bird visited the area on 23 April 1974. It was the first of several seen in Ireland in 1974.

SPOONBILL (*Platalea leucorodia*); vagrant
Two records: one was seen on the mudflats below Ballyscullion Demesne by the eminent ornithologist Peter Scott on 28 or 29 October 1937. Two were seen together from 25 May to at least 3 June 1975, on the west shore of the lough.

MALLARD (*Anas platyrhynchos*); resident, winter
   visitor and passage migrant
It is difficult to assess the number of breeding pairs of this duck, as many nest well back from the lough shore in the peripheral bogs and marshes. There are probably well over a hundred nesting in the area. One or two pairs have nested in the ivy-covered wall of the church on Church Island.

In late summer, a post-breeding flock of between two and three thousand is to be found on the lough, probably comprising local family parties, swollen by duck from Lough Neagh. This flock rarely exceeded a thousand until 1958, but has contained as many as 3,500, a count in late August, 1962.

In winter, the numbers rarely rise above five hundred, and may be well under one hundred in times of heavy shooting or high water level.

TEAL (*Anas crecca*); resident, winter visitor and
   passage migrant
Less than twenty pairs nest on the lough.

As a winter visitor, its numbers are generally around

The Heronry

a thousand, though fluctuating considerably with the intensity of shooting and the water level. The population is swollen in the early part of the year by migrants and by February and March up to 1,500 may be in the area.

By far the largest number of teal seen on the lough was 2,700 in March, 1965. This assemblage was considered to be due to immigration, probably from Britain, during a period of very cold easterly weather.

GREEN-WINGED TEAL (*Anas crecca carolinensis*); vagrant

A male showing the characters of this North American sub-species was observed amongst some common teal, near the north end of the lough, on 17 November 1968.

GARGANEY (*Anas querquedula*); rare passage migrant

This species has become more regular in recent years. It is usually seen singly or in pairs. A maximum of three (two drakes and a duck) was seen on 22 July 1967. It has been seen in the months from March to October inclusive. The maximum number of individuals to be seen in a year was seven in 1967.

The favourite location of the garganey at the lake is at Paddy's Dub.

GADWALL (*Anas strepera*); passage migrant and occasional winter visitor

This species occurs mainly on spring passage and generally in small numbers, although a maximum of twenty-six was seen in March 1960.

Other notable counts are sixteen on 21 October 1956, and fourteen on 29 January 1961.

The only summer record is of a drake on 28 June 1958.

It is possible that many gadwall by-pass Lough Beg on migration, as numbers to be seen in spring on the eastern shore of Lough Neagh (up to fifty in a day) are not reflected at Lough Beg.

BLUE-WINGED TEAL (*Anas discors*); vagrant

One record. One was shot on 30 September 1957. The wing was examined later (per C D Deane.)

WIGEON (*Anas penelope*); abundant winter visitor and passage migrant. It appears to be increasing.

The winter population was generally between one and two thousand. An influx often occurs towards the end of the winter, when numbers may be as high as 2,500. In recent years, the highest counts have been nearer 3,000.

Summer records are uncommon, but one or two summering birds would be easily overlooked in the large concentration of mallard. Three males (one adult and two immatures) were seen on 21 July 1956, and one male and two females on 22 July 1976. Other summer records have been of single birds.

The first autumn arrivals appear about the third week in August. Some late stayers remain on the lough well into May.

PINTAIL (*Anas acuta*); passage migrant, winter visitor and rare breeder

Numbers build up gradually throughout the winter, reaching a peak in February or March. Large numbers have, however, been occasionally noted in the winter months: 600 on 4 December 1955, and 450 on 16 December 1962. Nevertheless, the winter population is generally less than 200.

February figures for the five year period 1964 to 1968 average 490, whilst those of March for the same period average 520.

It should be noted that in the latter case, the average is somewhat distorted by the lough maximum of 940 pintail on 14 March 1965.

Breeding has long been suspected, but was not proved until 1959, when a nest with eight eggs was found. In 1967, three pintail broods were reared.

The pintail is one of the rarest breeding ducks in Ireland.

SHOVELER (*Anas clypeata*); passage migrant, winter visitor and breeder in small numbers

The main passage is in spring, numbers building up in February and reaching a peak in late February or March. Maximum spring numbers fluctuate from year to year, but are generally between two and four hundred. On occasions larger numbers have occurred, e.g. 550 on 15 February 1959, and 555 on 25 February 1968.

White Stork

G.D'A.

A pair of Gadwall

28

A similar build-up is normal in the autumn. Up until 1970, 200 was the normal figure in August and September. In recent years, however, (notably 1972 and 1976) up to 550 shoveler have been on the lough at this time. Although family parties of this species from the surrounding areas use the lake as a post-breeding resort, these large numbers must be composed mainly of early migrants. Good numbers may be found in October and November, e.g. 367 on 15 October 1967, and 400 on 12 October 1959.

The wintering population is around 100. The exceptional number of about 400 was counted on 4 December 1955.

Up to eleven pairs have bred on the Derry shore. In addition, a few pairs undoubtedly nest in the suitable habitat on the Antrim shore.

This duck is a localised breeder in Ireland, and Lough Beg must be regarded as one of its strongholds.

RED-CRESTED POCHARD (*Netta rufina*); vagrant
One record: a male was seen in a flock of 2,000 pochard on 1 January and 13 March 1966.

GOLDENEYE (*Bucephala clangula*); passage migrant and winter visitor
Thousands winter on Lough Neagh and many of these probably migrate through Lough Beg. This is especially noticeable in the early part of the year when birds are leaving the area en route to their Northern European breeding grounds. During this period, the regular winter population of under 100 is swollen to as many as 334 (5 April 1964). An exceptional count of 450 on 25 February 1956, probably represented a pre-departure built-up.

The first arrivals appear in October, and late migrants are still passing through in May. Late records are ten on 11 May 1963; six on 19 May 1975; forty on 13 May, eleven on 27 May, and five on 29 May 1976.

There are summer records of one on 21 June 1959,

and a flock of ten on 3 July 1976.

SCAUP (*Aythya marila*); irregular passage migrant and winter visitor
As this species favours large expanses of water, the flocks which migrate through, and winter on, the north western shore of Lough Neagh tend to by-pass Lough Beg. Small groups congregate in the Bann at Toome, mainly in the early months of the year.

On Lough Beg proper it occurs irregularly and in small parties. Eight were seen on 14 December 1955 and twelve on 13 May 1976.

A notable record was of a male on 3 June 1975.

TUFTED DUCK (*Aythya fuligula*); winter visitor, passage migrant and breeder
This species is generally the commonest diving duck on the lough, the largest numbers occurring in the winter. This population varies between one and three thousand. Considerable movement takes place between Lough Neagh and Lough Beg. On occasions, larger gatherings have been noted: 3,400 on 25 February 1956; 3,800 on 25 January 1958 and 25 February 1968.

Numbers are often as high as a thousand in the autumn, though an exceptional count was 1,100 as early as 31 August 1958.

Although Lough Beg was a breeding locality for this species as early as 1882, until 1958 only a few pairs bred. Since then, the breeding stock has been of the order of fifty pairs, the majority of which nest on the islets in the Lough.

POCHARD (*Aythya ferina*); winter visitor and passage migrant. Small numbers regularly summer but breeding has been proven only once.
When 1,000 were seen on 26 January 1958 and 1,600 on 26 October 1961, they were considered to be among the largest counts for this species in Ireland.

Since then, either through hard weather movement from Europe or, more probably, through a westerly shift in its normal wintering range, the pochard has become much more abundant.

They arrive 'en masse' often as early as late October, with up to 2,800 having been seen in that month. Largest numbers are to be found generally in November and December, the flocks tending to dissipate in the latter half of the winter. Since 1963 numbers of between two and four thousand have been normal in the November to January period. Occasionally huge concentrations, ie 5,500 in November 1967 and 7,600 in the same month in 1965, have been noted. The maximum for the lough was circa 8,000 on 12 December 1965.

Curiously, a high percentage of the wintering birds are males.

As with the previous species, there is considerable two-way traffic between the two loughs throughout the winter. In the latter part of the winter it is believed that the wintering Lough Beg pochard join up with the vast flocks on Lough Neagh before vacating the country.

A few pochard regularly summer at Lough Beg, and they seem to be increasing. A flock of fifty-one males was seen on 13 June 1975. Breeding has been suspected for many years (young were believed to have been shot on the lake in August 1878), but was not proven until August 1958 when a duck was seen with nine flightless young.

The pochard is a rare breeding duck in Ireland.

LONG-TAILED DUCK (*Clangula hyemalis*); rare winter visitor
There appear to be only three recent records: an immature male, 5 December 1954; two females, 4 December 1955; and one on 13 March 1966.

According to Ussher and Warren, this species was shot on more than one occasion at Lough Beg in the nineteenth century.

This species has occurred many times on Lough Neagh in the winter months, and it seems likely that it may visit Lough Beg unnoticed, more often than the records suggest.

COMMON SCOTER (*Melanitta nigra*) rare visitor
It has been recorded on three occasions. A pair remained at the sandpits from 26 May to 1 June 1963, and another pair was seen on 16 May 1964. Two males were observed on 1 March 1964.

RED-BREASTED MERGANSER (*Mergus serrator*); resident in small numbers
A few birds are present throughout the year.

Breeding was first proven in 1957 (two pairs) and since then it has bred regularly on a small scale. A maximum of five pairs nested in 1963.

GOOSANDER (*Mergus merganser*); rare visitor, mostly in the winter
The first record was of a pair on 2 October 1955. In 1963 two ducks appeared on 24 February, and on 3 March one drake and four ducks were seen on the lough. There have been isolated winter occurrences of single birds since then.

SMEW (*Mergus albellus*); vagrant
At least three records. One was shot at Toome, 22 February 1901. It was mounted by A Sheals and reported by the *Northern Whig* in January 1922. Single ducks were recorded on 18 April 1954, and from 2 December to the end of 1976.

The numerous records for Lough Neagh indicate that this species, especially the less conspicuous females, may occur more often on Lough Beg.

SHELDUCK (*Tadorna tadorna*); summer resident
The summer population is about forty birds, with up

to fifteen pairs breeding. Higher counts include eighty-two, mostly juveniles, on 28 June 1958; about sixty on 9 March 1963; seventy in March 1965, and seventy on 27 May 1976.

After the breeding season, the numbers fall off gradually, and it is unusual to see any by the onset of winter.

It is interesting to speculate about the shelduck's movements after the breeding season. The maritime loughs have wintering populations of this species, with up to a thousand on Belfast Lough, and smaller numbers on the others. It seems probable that the combined breeding populations of the lakes of the Lough Neagh basin winter on the coast to the east.

In 1976, a pair bred in a disused rabbit burrow at the roadside, almost half a mile away from the northern end of the lough.

BARNACLE GOOSE (*Branta leucopsis*); vagrant
A single record: one, which first appeared on 25 August 1975, stayed until the new year, 1976. Although apparently wild, the early date of initial observation suggests the possibility of escape from a wildfowl collection.

GREY-LAG GOOSE (*Anser anser*); regular passage migrant and winter visitor, generally in small numbers
This species is the commonest representative of the genus Anser on the lough. Flocks tend to be small, though twenty-nine were seen on 12 November 1967. Groups of less than a dozen are normal in winter and early spring. Some have lingered on until the start of May.

A small flock of this species has been seen grazing on the open fields in front of Ballyscullion House, in the winter.

It appears that geese were more common in the area in years gone by. I believe that with a lessening of shooting intensity this species would stay longer in the excellent habitat, and could perhaps be encouraged to build up a regular wintering population.

GREENLAND WHITE-FRONTED GOOSE (*Anser albifrons flavirostris*); passage migrant and winter visitor in small numbers
This species occurs less frequently than the previous species. Groups of six or more are fairly normal at times in the winter, or on passage.

The migratory flightline from its arctic breeding grounds to its main wintering place in Wexford has been shown to be an approximate NW/SE diagonal across Ireland. It is therefore understandably irregular in the Bann valley in any substantial numbers.

PINK-FOOTED GOOSE (*Anser brachyrhynchus*); rare passage migrant
It has been noted on a few occasions, mostly in the company of grey-lags.

The most recent occurrences were of one with a few grey-lags on several occasions in the winter of 1975/6, and a flock of eleven on 28 September 1976.

Two were shot out of a flock of twenty-three on 24 October 1959. They had been ringed as adults in Iceland in July 1953.

MUTE SWAN (*Cygnus olor*); resident
Probably up to about twenty-five pairs breed on small islands on the east and west shores and at the sandpits.

There is also a non-breeding population of around 200 resident throughout the year. In winter, 300 may be on the lough due to 'hard weather' movement. An excessively high count was 370 on 25 February 1956.

WHOOPER SWAN (*Cygnus cygnus*); winter visitor, passage migrant and regular summerer in very small numbers
These swans arrive in bulk in October, build up to a

G. D'A.

Pink-footed Geese

wintering population of around 300, and depart northwards again, mainly in April. This is one of the largest wintering flocks of whoopers in the north of Ireland, and on occasions it has been swollen by as much as 50%: circa 450 were present in December 1962.

March counts tend to be the highest, with passage migrants from further south joining up with the wintering birds.

Migration not only takes place in a north/south orientation, but also to and from the north west. Parties of whoopers have been seen departing in the

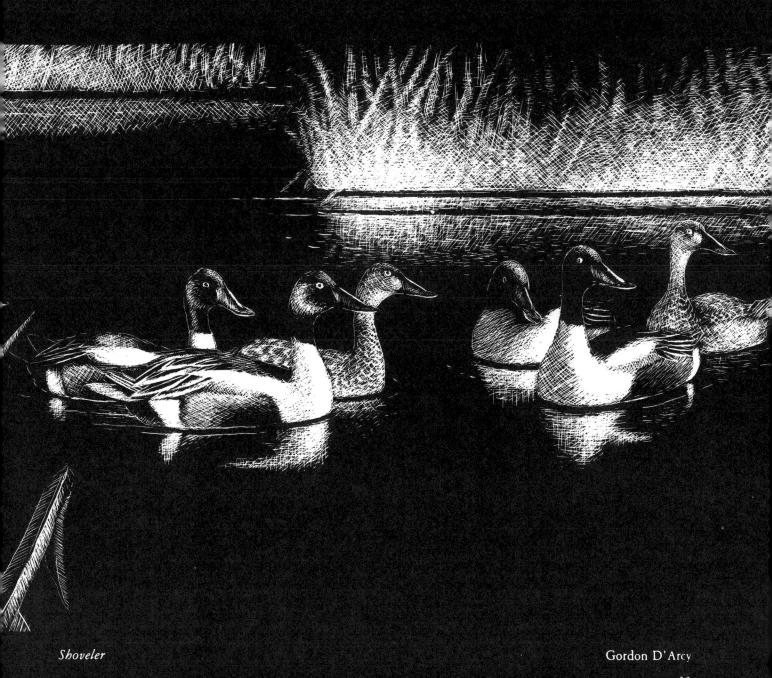

Shoveler

Gordon D'Arcy

A pair of Tufted Duck

Gordon D'Arcy

34

A flight of Goldeneye

Gordon D'Arcy

A pair of Smew

36

direction of the Sperrins, probably en route to other 'stop-off' areas like Lough Foyle. These departures often take place on clear evenings in March or April.

A small number of whooper swans, usually less than five, regularly summer at the lough. Breeding has never been proven, but in 1963 an adult whooper was seen sitting on a mute swan's nest during the breeding season.

Immature birds compose a small fraction, usually about 10% of the flocks.

In times of flooding, whoopers take to the fields, when they may be seen in the open land of the Creagh.

During the 1939-45 war, whooper swans were shot on Lough Beg and sold in Ballymena for ten shillings per bird. They were not only used as food, but it was said that their skins were used for the manufacture of ladies' purses.

BEWICK'S SWAN (*Cygnus bewickii*); winter visitor and passage migrant in late winter

The numbers rarely approach those of the former species, but in hard weather it can occur in substantial flocks. Until 1964, there were rarely more than 100 bewicks, except for 117 on 18 March 1956, and 106 on 22 December 1963.

In 1964, the numbers built up in the following fashion:

1 January	169
5 January	125
19 January	45
26 January	128
1 February	35
8 February	105
16 February	245
20 February	231
23 February	239
1 March	215

In the last ten years, winter figures have again been seldom in excess of 100.

Summer records are scarce. They include one on 12 August 1956; one all June 1961; one June to August 1963, joined by two more on 1 September; one on 29 July 1967.

The percentage of immatures tends to be higher in this species than in the former — often 15%-40%.

SPARROW HAWK (*Accipiter nisus*); resident in the woods on both sides of Lough Beg

Up until 1960, two pairs bred in the area. Between 1961 and 1963, breeding apparently ceased and there were few sightings. Since then the sparrow hawk has recovered and is probably more common now than before. I suspect that at least three pairs are nesting in the area (summer 1976) though the evidence is circumstantial.

Sparrow hawks are common in the autumn at Lough Beg. It could be that these are locally reared birds, or perhaps migrants from outside the area.

GOSHAWK (*Accipiter gentilis*); vagrant

Once recorded; an adult female was seen on 12 August 1956, and probably the same bird again on 16 September of the same year.

HEN HARRIER (*Circus cycanus*); uncommon visitor.

Single birds are occasionally seen in the autumn or winter, hunting over the meadows. It has also been seen at the sandpits and in the low-lying arable fields of the Creagh.

As this species increases in Northern Ireland, it may become a more frequent visitor to the ideal habitat at Lough Beg.

OSPREY (*Pandion haliaetus*); vagrant

The first record is of one seen catching fish on the lough on 25 April 1976.

Hen Harrier

There is an unsubtantiated sighting of one seen by local fishermen in the first week of July 1974. Although it was not officially recorded, it was well seen and raised considerable attention at the time.

PEREGRINE FALCON (*Falco peregrinus*); previously a rare visitor: in recent years sightings have increased

An adult male on 22 October 1955 was the only record for many years. Over the past few years, however, there have been many sightings, mostly in the winter.

Carcasses of medium sized birds like teal have been found, obviously killed by a predatory bird. This suggests that peregrines may be regular visitors to the area.

MERLIN (*Falco columbarius*); regular visitor, mostly on passage

Singles are identified from time to time at the lake.

Next to the sparrow hawk and the kestrel, it is the most regularly occurring bird of prey.

From my experience, the merlin is more frequent in the autumn than at any other time, and is especially fond of hunting in the meadows on the western side. I suspect that individuals wander to the lough from the Sperrins.

KESTREL (*Falco tinnunculus*); resident

The most frequently observed raptor in the area. At least two pairs nest. It is most often seen hunting in the arable land around the lough in numbers of up to six in a day. There is no indication of migration through the lough.

PARTRIDGE (*Perdix perdix*)

Donaldson and Watson (1963) considered the partridge to be a scarce resident: 'Odd parties seen in

Peregrine Falcon chasing a Knot

the surrounding fields and rough ground.'

A small covey was seen feeding at the verge of one of the lanes in the Creagh some ten years ago.

I, however, have not been fortunate enough to see this species at Lough Beg. If it is still to be found, it must be extremely local. Local people are of the opinion that, although the partridge is still to be found within a twenty mile radius of the area, it is no longer at Lough Beg.

PHEASANT (*Phasianus colchicus*); resident; numbers have fallen off in recent years

Small numbers of pheasants were to be found in the overgrown bogs and bracken-covered areas around the lough. It was also seen in the Ballyscullion Estate.

It has decreased considerably in the past ten years, probably due to intensive shooting.

CRANE (*Grus grus*); vagrant

One record. One was shot on 24 July 1958, and the

carcass examined on the 31st of the month. Although escape from captivity cannot be ruled out in this case, the indications are that the bird was a common crane, *megalornis grus*, and therefore more likely to be a genuine straggler from Europe.

WATER RAIL (*Rallus aquaticus*); scarce resident

Due to the very skulking behaviour of this species, its exact status in the lough is uncertain.

It probably breeds in the suitable habitat at the south end of the lough, where it has been heard calling at times. It was seen there on 17 August 1958, and an adult was seen with young in summer 1972.

• The most recent sighting was on the west shore, near Coney Island, on 18 August 1976.

It has also been heard at a marsh at Toome. Due to development, however, this habitat no longer exists in its original form.

There are ideal habitats for this species on the Antrim shore of the lough, but its presence there has yet to be detected.

CORNCRAKE (*Crex crex*); scarce summer visitor

Formerly widespread in the area, its numbers have steadily declined, probably due to modern agricultural methods.

In 1963, a few were still to be found in the south and west, but the unmistakeable call is uncommon anywhere now.

The first arrivals are in early April. The most recent spring sighting was of one seen on 23 April 1976. It may still be found in the area adjoining the west side of the Bann, just north of Toome.

WATERHEN (*Gallinula chloropus*); resident

The majority are found in the quieter reed-fringed ponds in the sandpits, where many pairs breed. Pairs are to be found scattered along the Antrim shore in suitable habitats and isolated breeding occurs also in a few places along the western shore. It is not restricted to the lough itself, many being found in the ditches and boggy hollows well back from the lake.

There appears to be little fluctuation in the population throughout the year, though in winter this bird is sometimes seen in fields and along lanes, often at some distance from water.

COOT (*Fulica atra*); resident, passage migrant and winter visitor

Probably at least forty pairs breed, mainly along the Antrim shore and in the sandpits. On the western shore it breeds on the smaller islands.

The winter population is generally around 200, though on occasions up to 700 have been seen.

The coot is an abundant passage migrant in the autumn at Lough Beg. This movement was first noted in 1955, when on 9 October a thousand were seen. In 1967 the figures were as follows:

17 September	1,310
15 October	1,240
12 November	1,230

In 1968:

18 August	700
22 September	2,000
20 October	1,400
17 November	800

Peak figures are evident on Lough Neagh in late autumn and vast congregations have been noted on lakes in Westmeath and Galway in the same period.

OYSTERCATCHER (*Haematopus ostralegus*); scarce summer resident and passage migrant

Usually one or two pairs breed in the area. A maximum of three nests with eggs was found in 1963. This is one of the few inland breeding sites of the

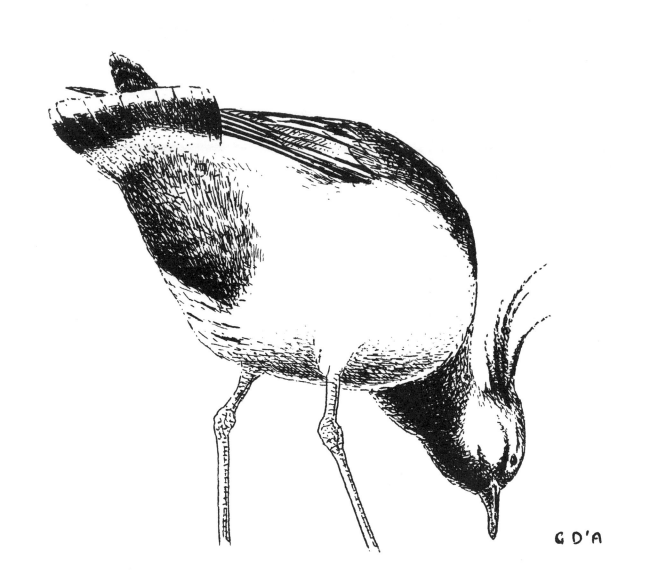

GD'A

Lapwing

oystercatcher in Northern Ireland.

On passage, it is commoner in the autumn, when small numbers may be seen. A maximum of eleven was noted on 9 August 1963. Exceptional spring numbers were seven on 15 March 1964, and nine on 2 April of the same year.

LAPWING (*Vanellus vanellus*); resident, passage
    migrant and winter visitor in large numbers
Up to forty pairs breed at present. After the severe winter of 1962/3, only about ten to twelve pairs nested.

The numbers build up in late summer with post-breeding lapwings converging on the meadows from surrounding areas. Up to 1,000 may be found in the area in late August or early September. Winter immigrants appear in October, the winter population varying from a couple of hundred to around a thousand.

Usually, the largest numbers are to be found in the months of January and February, when up to 2,000 have been noted. However, 2,000 were present in November and December 1975.

RINGED PLOVER (*Charadrius hiaticula*); passage
    migrant and summer resident in small numbers
In most years a few pairs breed at the sandpits. The main passage is in the spring. Build-up of this species is to some extent dependent on the amount of mud exposed by the fluctuating water level. The largest spring counts are fifty-five on 11 May 1965, and eighty-nine on 31 May 1960.

Smaller numbers pass through in the autumn with a normal daily total of less than twenty. An unusual autumn count was sixty on 10 September 1962.

Although uncommon in winter, three were seen on 16 February 1964.

GREY-PLOVER (*Pluvialis squatarola*); irregular passage migrant
Since it was first noticed on 3 April 1961, this species has made irregular appearances mostly in the autumn and sometimes in startling numbers.

In autumn 1962, grey plovers were seen in unprecedented numbers for an inland lake. Passage took place from early September to late October, with a peak of thirty-three on 28 October.

Passage in autumn 1963 was on a smaller scale, with a peak of six on 1 October.

The volume of passage has considerably diminished and been more erratic since then.

Birds seen in the spring have been in summer plumage, as were three on 31 May 1964.

GOLDEN PLOVER (*Pluvialis apricaria*); abundant
    passage migrant and winter visitor
The first migrants generally appear in the latter half of August. Numbers then build up steadily until the wintering population of around 1,000 is present, in November.

Spring passage swells the numbers to several thousands. The maximum count was at least 5,000 on 5 March 1961. These flocks build up on the meadows in March and April, and fly off in groups in suitable weather conditions. By the start of May, very few are left at the lough.

Both northern and southern forms of the species are represented. A flock of some 2,500 on 18 April 1976, was at least 75% northern sub-species.

Departing birds have been observed flying north-west towards the Sperrins.

Summering records are rare, but one of the northern form did summer at the lough in 1975.

TURNSTONE (*Arenaria interpres*); scarce passage
    migrant
Most records are for the autumn. It has been recorded in May, July, August, September and October, usually

Dowitcher

in ones or twos. Exceptional counts were five on 8 September 1957, and eight on 6 September 1964.

Summer birds have appeared in full plumage on the lough.

DOWITCHER (*Limnodromus scolopaceus/griseus*); vagrant

Has been recorded three times. One was seen on numerous occasions between 28 October 1961, and 28 January 1962. A second was seen on 2 October 1963, and remained until 13 October. The third was seen in late autumn about 1970 (exact date unknown). All were considered to be long-billed dowitchers.

The bird of 1961 commuted between Loughs Neagh and Beg and both the earlier birds associated with golden plover on the open meadows.

SNIPE (*Capella gallinago*); resident, passage migrant and winter visitor

Probably about twenty pairs breed, but nests are difficult to find, and may be underestimated.

The largest passage takes place in the autumn, with many counts of between 100 and 200 in a day. In winter, the numbers are seldom as high as 100, an exceptional count being at least 114 on 22 December 1963.

On passage, snipe can sometimes be seen feeding on the open mud on the west shore of the lough.

JACK SNIPE (*Lymnocryptes minimus*); passage migrant and winter visitor

First arrivals generally appear in September, and last birds are found in April. Throughout the winter, single birds may be flushed from the less disturbed marshy areas on the south and west shores.

Daily totals are invariably small, the highest being seven on 22 October 1961.

An early arrival was one on 22 August 1963.

WOODCOCK (*Scolopax rusticola*); resident and winter visitor in small numbers

Up to three pairs have been noticed in summer.

Due to the gradual clearance of the willow and alder woods in the low-lying boggy areas, much of the habitat previously occupied by woodcocks has been destroyed. Should this trend continue, this species is in danger of extinction in the area.

It is found in some of the woodland in the Bally-scullion Demesne. It breeds along the wooded Antrim shore, in small numbers, and near Toome.

CURLEW (*Numenius arquata*); resident
Probably about ten pairs breed with a few more nesting in the surrounding area. In May and June a flock of 50-70 gathers by the lake shore in the evening.

Small flocks occasionally turn up on passage or during the winter, but numbers rarely rise above 100.

WHIMBREL (*Numenius phaeopus*); passage migrant, commonest in spring
This species undoubtedly uses the valley of the upper Bann as a flight line on migration. In the months of April and May flocks fly into the lough from the south, often continuing due north without stopping. Groups of about six are regular but the following high counts have been noted:

    30 on 8 May 1960
    2 flocks totalling 56 on 26 April 1962
    36 on 12 May 1963
    28 on 19 May 1963
    One flock of 93 on 23 April 1976
    60 on 25 April 1976

In autumn the whimbrel is less notable, usually seen singly or in small parties.

An exceptional count was a southward bound flock of thirty-five on 23 August 1963.

BLACK-TAILED GODWIT (*Limosa limosa*); passage migrant, mainly in spring
The first migrants arrive in February, often in the early part of the month, but the main movement is in March and early April. It is possibly increasing in numbers. The peaks in 1956 and 1957 were 142 and 130 respectively, whilst 343 and 521 were peaks for 1959 and 1963. The figure for 1963 is, however, the maximum total for a day and although spring counts of 300 or more are normal, any total approaching 500 is exceptional.

In the autumn, it is unusual to see more than twenty in a day.

Summering has been more frequent in recent years, with a maximum of 113 in 1962. Smaller numbers also summered in the years 1961-1964 inclusive.

This species is one of the 'classical' migrants through Lough Beg. It breeds in Iceland and many use the valley of the Lower Bann as a flightline in spring from its main wintering grounds in southern Ireland.

BAR-TAILED GODWIT (*Limosa lapponica*); uncommon migrant, mainly in the autumn
It was first recorded on 8 August 1957. Since then it has been seen singly or in small groups in most years.

In autumn 1963, a clear passage involving quite a number of birds took place. One appeared on 20 July and numbers built up to a peak of sixteen on 15 September, falling to ten on 5 October, and gradually disappearing thereafter. The maximum was twenty-one on 26 July 1964.

In spring, three were seen on 27 March 1959. A single bar-tail was seen on 7 June 1964.

GREEN SANDPIPER (*Tringa ochropus*); regular autumn migrant in small numbers
It was first recorded on 31 May 1953. Three were seen on 1 June 1963 and these two records constitute the birds' status in spring at Lough Beg.

One or two are seen in most autumns, usually in August or early September. Altogether eight were seen in 1963, including a small passage of five birds towards the end of August. These birds were watched flying south in the evening, stopping only momentarily on the lough.

G. D'A.

Green Sandpiper

WOOD SANDPIPER (*Tringa glareola*); regular
autumn migrant in small numbers
It has occurred more or less annually since it was first
recorded on 24 August 1961.

In 1963 a passage occurred in both spring and
autumn, involving as many as six birds on 13 June and
17 September. In 1966 a total of five were seen
between 13 August and 28 August.

It has been seen on the lough in every month from
May to October inclusive.

The wood sandpiper appears to be more regular
than the green sandpiper at Lough Beg.

COMMON SANDPIPER (*Tringa hypoleucos*); passage
migrant and summer resident in small numbers
A few pairs (up to five) used to nest regularly. It has,
however, declined as a breeding species, and may be
on the verge of extinction at the lough.

Both breeding birds and migrants have passed
through by mid-September. The peak passage takes
place in late July and early August. A maximum of
twenty-four birds was seen on 23 July 1963.

The only winter record is of a single bird on 21
February 1959.

REDSHANK (*Tringa totanus*); common passage
migrant and summer resident
The summer birds begin to arrive in early February,
and the breeding stock has moved out by late July.
These are followed by passage migrants in late
autumn.

Between thirty-five and forty-five pairs are present
in the breeding season, and in general at least twenty-
five pairs breed. It is not unusual to see over a
hundred redshank in spring on the lough. The
maximum daily total is 160.

Although uncommon in the winter, thirteen were
seen on 8 December, and three on 15 December 1963.

SPOTTED REDSHANK (*Tringa erythropus*); regular
autumn passage migrant, uncommon in the spring
In the autumn, birds arrive first in early August, reach
a peak, generally in September, and tail off in
October. It is unusual to see any by November.
Numbers are generally small, groups of up to six
together being normal. However, nine were seen on 1
September 1963, and ten, including a flock of about
eight, on 30 August 1976.

This species has probably been seen less than a
dozen times in spring and only in ones or twos. It has
been recorded, though, in March, April, May and
June, and has been seen in the black, full summer
plumage.

In recent years, it has increased in numbers and
regularity.

GREATER YELLOWLEGS (*Tringa melanleuca*);
vagrant
One record: a bird was seen on 22 September 1962. It
is considered probable that the individual concerned
was the same one that was at the north end of Lough
Neagh on 2 September 1962.

LESSER YELLOWLEGS (*Tringa flavipes*); vagrant
A single record: one was seen on 24 May 1958. This
was the second Irish record of this American species.

GREENSHANK (*Tringa nebularia*); passage migrant
Small numbers pass through in the spring months of
March, April, and May, rarely more than five or six in
a day.

In the autumn, however, significant numbers start
to appear at the end of July, and continue to move
through till October, in numbers of up to about
twenty in a day.

The maximum seen in a day was forty-two on
2 September 1962.

Winter records are few, but one was seen on several

Whooper Swans

Gordon D'Arcy

Bewick's Swans

Gordon D'Arcy

Coots

Gordon D'Arcy

49

Black-tailed Godwits

Gordon D'Arcy

G. D'A.

Spotted Redshanks

occasions throughout the winter of 1963/64.

There are also a few summer records.

KNOT (*Calidris canutus*); regular autumnal passage
migrant

This species, generally considered rare inland, has,
however, in recent years become a habitual migrant to

the area. The numbers vary from year to year but a
dozen on a day, from August to October, is normal.
On occasions unprecedented numbers have been seen,
twenty-four on 8 September 1957, and forty-eight on
20 August 1960.

Spring records are rare, about half a dozen in all,
but it has been seen in March, April, May and June.

On 13 May 1976 a flock comprising some seventy birds flew into Lough Beg across the Creagh from the south, and proceeded directly north, along the western shore and out of the area, without stopping.

Three were seen on 25 January 1964.

LITTLE STINT (*Calidris minuta*); regular passage migrant in small numbers

This species was first recorded on the lough in 1961, but has since become a regular migrant, mainly in the autumn. It occurs in small parties, an exceptional count being eight on 15 September 1975.

It has been recorded in April, May and June, though usually singly. In spring 1976 however, three were present most of April and May, with a peak of five on 30 April.

One was seen on 2 July 1961, an unusual date for the species in Ireland.

WHITE-RUMPED SANDPIPER (*Calidris fuscicollos*); vagrant

One record: one was seen on 21 October 1956. This is regarded as the second definite Irish record of this American wader.

PECTORAL SANDPIPER (*Calidris melanotos*); rare, though probably annual, visitor

Since it was first seen in 1961, the pectoral sandpiper has been seen almost every autumn, usually singly, but in numbers of up to three together. The favoured months are September and October, but early stragglers have been seen in August and late ones in November.

There is a record of a single bird on 1 June 1963, which was present until the 15th of the month.

At least four individuals were observed in the years 1961 and 1963. This arctic American wader is probably as likely to appear at Lough Beg in the autumn as anywhere else in Ireland.

DUNLIN (*Calidris alpina*); common passage migrant, winter visitor and breeder in small numbers

Generally less than a dozen pairs nest, but in 1963 at least fifteen pairs did. Around twenty to forty non-breeding birds summer in the area, mostly at Paddy's Dub.

As a passage migrant and winter visitor, it appears to be increasing. Numbers of the order of sixty to a hundred are normal in late autumn, but up to 120 have been noted.

In winter, this species congregates with the golden plovers. Up to 1963, forty-four was considered a large count, but in recent years I have seen it in hundreds, including at least 400 in late autumn, 1974.

CURLEW SANDPIPER (*Calidris ferruginea*); regular passage migrant in small numbers

It was first recorded on 20 August 1960. In 1961, a small passage was noted, with a maximum of three individuals on 28 October. A similar movement occurred in 1963, though with a peak of only five on 2 October.

The passage in 1975 reached a maximum, on 9 September, of fifteen birds.

There is a winter record, a single bird on 12 December 1965.

BUFF-BREASTED SANDPIPER (*Tryngites subruficollis*); rare autumn visitor (once in late spring)

The first record was one on 13 August to 23 September 1961. In 1963 one was seen on 1 June, and another on 25 September. There are autumn records also for 1968, 1974, and 1975 of single birds: 8 October 1968; 13-27 September 1974, and 25 August 1975.

The unprecedented total of five together was present most of September and October 1975.

This species shows an affinity to the golden plover, spending most of its time in the open meadows.

Pectoral Sandpiper

G. D'A.

BAIRD'S SANDPIPER (*Calidris bairdii*); vagrant
Once recorded. On 15 September 1975, one was seen in the company of dunlins and little stints near Church Island.

BROAD-BILLED SANDPIPER (*Limicola falcinellus*); vagrant
A single record. One was observed on 15 and 16 June 1963, during a period when a number of rare waders had appeared on the lough. One had already been seen in Belfast Lough on 11 May of the same year.

The Lough Beg bird was the third Irish record for this northern European species.

SANDERLING (*Calidris alba*); occasional visitor on migration
The sanderling is a fairly regular migrant, in spring and autumn, to the north shore of Lough Neagh. The numbers are generally small, but up to twenty have been seen there.

On Lough Beg proper, it has been seen on a very few occasions in spring and autumn. There are three records for 1964: single birds on 16 and 31 May, and five on 1 August.

RUFF (*Philomachus pugnax*); passage migrant
The largest numbers occur in the autumn, from the middle of August to the start of October, with a peak generally in early September.

Since 1961 it has become increasingly more common, the maxima rising from ten to ninety. The average maximum is, however, thirty to forty. By the start of October the numbers diminish and only small groups continue to pass through by the start of November.

Although regular on spring passage the numbers are invariably small, more than four being notable. The males in the spring are often in breeding plumage and ruffs of a wide diversity of colour and pattern have

been seen. Display behaviour has also been seen at the lough.

It has been recorded in every month of the year but less so in June, July and from December to March. However, wintering has occurred in several years: the maximum was eleven, present from October to March 1962.

GREY PHALAROPE (*Phalaropus fulicarius*); vagrant
Two records. One was shot on 18 October 1891, and another was shot by Colonel Bruce about five years before this.

WILSON'S PHALAROPE (*Phalaropus tricolor*); vagrant
Recorded once. A bird in winter plumage was seen on 7 and 9 September 1975.

ARCTIC SKUA (*Stercorarius parasiticus*); vagrant
One, accompanied by common terns, was seen flying north along Lough Beg on 11 June 1894.

GREAT BLACK-BACKED GULL (*Larus marinus*) non-breeding resident
Although the numbers are highest in summer, this gull is present throughout the year in small numbers. Up to 100 have been seen, but generally less than a dozen in a day is normal.

LESSER BLACK-BACKED GULL (*Larus fuscus graellsii*); passage migrant and summer visitor
Small numbers only are to be expected at Lough Beg. A fairly static population is to be found at the eel-fishery at Toome. It is probable that the numbers are governed by the breeding population on Lough Neagh. Fifty to a hundred are normal at the eel-fishery in spring and summer.

HERRING GULL (*Larus argentatus*); non-breeding

Great Black-Backed Gull

resident

This species is present throughout the year in widely varying numbers. Up to 300 have been seen in a day.

In the summer months, a large percentage of immatures is to be found.

COMMON GULL (*Larus canus*); regular visitor in small numbers

One or two may be seen on any day in the year. There seems to be no pattern, the occurrences appearing to be mainly of a random nature.

An exceptional count was of seventeen on 17 August 1963.

GLAUCOUS GULL (*Larus hyperboreus*); vagrant to the area

Two records. A first winter bird was found dead at the sandpits on 18 January 1964. A sub-adult was seen on 19 May 1968.

There are several records for this species on Lough Neagh.

ICELAND GULL (*Larus glaucoides*); vagrant to the area
A single record: one was found dead on 20 April 1903.

This northern species, like the glaucous gull, is rare outside its maritime environment.

LITTLE GULL (*Larus minutus*); irregular spring visitor
All the records are of immatures.

The first record was of a single bird on 15 May 1955. Another was recorded on 1 May 1965.

In 1968, two immatures were seen on 19 May, followed by four on 15 June. In 1972, two were seen on 14 May, and in 1973, a single on 1 June.

There may be more occurrences, as little gulls could be easily overlooked amongst the masses of breeding black-headed gulls.

BLACK-HEADED GULL (*Larus ridibundus*); resident
It breeds abundantly on four islands on the lough. The total population is of the order of 600 to 750 breeding pairs, but has decreased in the past fifteen years, due perhaps to increasing disturbance. At least half of the total is found on Dewhamill Island, immediately north of Church Island. In 1961 high water level forced many of the gulls to nest in the rushes on the meadows, but the success rate was very low, due to pillaging by scavengers like hooded crows and magpies.

There may be as many as 2,500 black-headed gulls in the area in early April and similar numbers in late summer. In the autumn, dispersal takes place towards the coast and much smaller numbers remain throughout the winter.

KITTIWAKE (*Rissa tridactyla*); rare inland
Three records. Two have been found dead, one on 7 March 1963, and one on 16 February 1964. An adult was seen on 15 December 1963.

BLACK TERN (*Chlidonias niger*); erratic autumnal passage migrant
Most of the records have been in September and October.

The first recording was of seven on 9 September 1954. A considerable passage in 1955 peaked with sixteen on 25 September.

Singles were observed in 1957 and 1961, and small numbers have been seen in several of the years since then.

The most recent significant passage was of up to six from 8 to 21 September 1974.

COMMON TERN (*Sterna hirundo*); summer visitor
For many years, there has been a breeding colony on one of the islands in the sandpits. It appears that the number of breeding pairs is diminishing. At its maximum in 1958, it comprised twenty-one nests. In 1963, the average was estimated at ten nests, but at present only about five pairs are to be found breeding there.

It has been suggested that nesting may have occurred on Dewhamill Island in years gone by.

LITTLE TERN (*Sterna albifrons*); rare inland
One record: a single bird was seen on 2 July 1961.

SANDWICH TERN (*Sterna sandvicencis*); rare inland
Two records. The first inland record for Northern Ireland, apart from the breeding colony on Lower Lough Erne, was one on 28 June 1958. The other was of a bird on 26 July 1975.

STOCK DOVE (*Columba oenas*); resident
Breeding was first proved in 1962 and probably continues in small numbers.

Most are found in the spring and summer, when up to thirty may be seen in a day.

In the winter, small numbers occur in the arable

Collared Dove

fields.

This dove is much less gregarious than the following species, and tends to mix little with it.

WOODPIGEON (*Columba palumbus*); resident
This species breeds abundantly in the wooded areas surrounding the lough.

In the winter large numbers are to be found, the breeding stock being swollen by immigrants. A winter roost of some three thousand birds exists in one of the woods at the western side of the area.

COLLARED DOVE (*Streptopelia decaocto*); resident
Donaldson and Watson recorded this dove as a rare visitor in 1963. Since the first recording on 9 June of that year, it has increased to the status of an abundant resident, mainly at the farms and at Toome.

CUCKOO (*Cuculus canorus*); summer visitor
The first cuckoos of the year at Lough Beg are heard with unusual regularity in the third week of April.

Up to nine have been noted in the area in a day. One of the rare 'red' phase was seen on Coney Island on 25 August 1975.

BARN OWL (*Tyto alba*); has bred
In the past, it has bred in Toome and is well known there. Although it is locally believed that barn owls are found in the vicinity of the ruined church on Church Island, this has yet to be substantiated. It has, however, been seen hunting at duck on occasions, in the area of the lough.

A 'white owl', probably of this species, was shot at the lough in winter 1962.

LONG-EARED OWL (*Asio otus*); local resident
Breeding was first proved in 1963 with the discovery of a nest containing one egg and two fledglings.

There are probably a few pairs breeding, possibly on

both shores, but their nocturnal habits make these owls difficult to locate.

SHORT-EARED OWL (*Asio flammeus*); winter visitor in very small numbers
One or two probably spend the winter at the lough in most years.

It has been noted as early as August and a maximum for one day was three on 15 October 1961.

NIGHTJAR (*Caprimulgus europaeus*); rare summer visitor
Breeding was proven in 1960 when a nest with two eggs was found in 'Ballyscullion Moss' — the raised peat bog on the eastern side of Lough Beg.

Nightjars have been noticed in the same locality on a number of occasions since 1960 indicating that it may nest there regularly.

This rare and most interesting species may nest in other suitable habitat near the lake but due to its crepuscular nature, the exact status is difficult to determine.

SWIFT (*Apus apus*); passage migrant and summer visitor
The first arrivals are generally at the beginning of May and the species is abundant in the area by the end of the month. Very few remain till September. An early record was two on 21 April 1963.

Breeding takes place in a few locations, including the Church steeple on Church Island, and on one or two buildings at Toome. Only a few pairs are involved.

In the summer months, large concentrations of swifts have been noticed. Those in June and July are probably simply feeding on the insect swarms which plague the area at that time, whilst those in August may be departing migrants. Two thousand on 18 June, and 8,000 on 25 June 1961, probably represent

Displaying Nightjar

feeding accumulations of the species.

A pre-migration build up of some 1,300 swifts was noted on 10 August 1963.

SWALLOW (*Hirundo rustica*); summer visitor and passage migrant

Many pairs breed in the farms throughout the area. They arrive in early April and depart in September. Late stayers have been seen in the third week of October. The lough acts as a magnet to southward bound swallows in late summer. Up to 3,000 gathered at the lake in the evenings in August 1976.

Swallows ringed as nestlings at a farm on the west side of the lake were trapped in the same barn the following year.

HOUSE MARTIN (*Delichon urbica*); summer visitor and passage migrant

First arrivals are generally towards the end of April, departures in September.

A colony exists at Toome, and others breed in scattered buildings near the lake.

Numbers are generally small, but over a hundred have been seen in a day.

Thompson found a numerous settlement of this species under the arches of Toome Bridge in the nineteenth century.

SAND MARTIN (*Riparia riparia*); summer visitor and passage migrant

A colony exists in the sandpits, which usually comprises some 200 pairs, but up to 500 pairs have nested there. A few have nested in the sandy face of the diatomite cuttings near Toome.

The first birds arrive at the lough at the start of April, departing in August and September.

Pre-migratory gatherings may be large, frequently hundreds. A maximum of 1,000 was seen on 28 July 1957.

The previous earliest sighting was of one at Church Island on 24 March 1975; however two were seen together near the Annagh on 13 March 1977.

KINGFISHER (*Alcedo atthis*); local resident

One or two pairs nest in the bank of the River Bann between Toome and Lough Beg. After the severe winter of 1962/3 none were seen for a while, but it has since become re-established.

Deane states that kingfishers have occasionally been found drowned in the eel coghill nets at Toome.

I have seen the species away from its normal river habitat, on the small islands on the western shore of the lake. Due to frequent sightings in the marshes on the Antrim shore, there is a possibility that it may nest in one of the small streams which flow into the lough from the east.

GREAT-SPOTTED WOODPECKER (*Dendrocopus major*); vagrant

One recording of a single bird at Toome, early 1969. It occurred at a time when there was a minor invasion of the species in Ireland.

SKYLARK (*Alauda arvensis*); resident, passage migrant and winter visitor

Many pairs nest in the open meadows and in the less disturbed arable fields of the neighbourhood. Flocks appear in the meadows in the autumn, which may be composed, in part, of locally reared larks. Migrants however undoubtedly pass through as up to fifty may be seen in October-November and March-April.

Larger flocks occur in the winter, especially in the latter half. Up to 200 have been seen in the sandpits during February.

RAVEN (*Corvus corax*); rare visitor

I am aware of only two definite occurrences, one on 16 February 1956, and one in winter 1972/3 (exact date

Wilson's Phalarope

Gordon D'Arcy

Arctic Skua and Common Tern

Gordon D'Arcy

Gull Colony, Dewhamill Island

Gordon D'Arcy

63

Short-eared Owl

Gordon D'Arcy

64

unknown).

This species probably occasionally wanders to the lough, outside the breeding season, from the Sperrin mountains.

CARRION CROW (*Corvus corone*); rare visitor
It does not appear to breed in the area, but turns up in ones and twos in most years.

HOODED CROW (*Corvus cornix*); resident
Several pairs nest in the area.

Many descend on the lough in spring and summer, egg-hunting from the breeding waders, gulls and ducks. Judging from the number of empty shells to be found, these crows must be regarded as a major hazard to the success of the hapless ground-nesters of the lough. Up to a hundred hoodies, accompanied by similar numbers of jackdaws, habitually indulge in this activity.

In winter, thirty is a normal figure, but sixty-six were seen on 15 December 1963.

ROOK (*Corvus frugilegus*); resident
A large rookery exists in the woods of the Ballyscullion Demesne. In winter, flocks are to be found in the open land near the lough shore.

JACKDAW (*Corvus monedula*); resident
A fair number breed in the old buildings in the area, especially in the ruined church on Church Island.

Rooks and jackdaws accumulate in feeding flocks in the winter. An exceptional gathering on 15 December 1963 numbered around 1,400 and may have been composed, at least in part, of immigrants.

MAGPIE (*Pica pica*); resident
Many pairs breed.

Magpies indulge in nest-robbing, though to a much lesser degree than the hooded crows. Although common, they have not yet reached 'pest' proportions at Lough Beg.

Numbers remain fairly static all year round.

JAY (*Garrulus glandarius*); formerly a local resident
Until the 1940s it was found in the Ballyscullion Demesne in small numbers. Lady Mulholland has observed it only once or twice since then.

It appears to be established in the Moyola Estate at Castledawson, a few miles to the west of Lough Beg.

GREAT TIT (*Parus major*); resident
A small breeding population exists in the surrounding woodland.

BLUE TIT (*Parus caeruleus*); resident
The commonest member of the tit family in the area, it is a widespread breeder in suitable locations.

In the late autumn and winter, foraging flocks of this species may be encountered in various parts.

COAL TIT (*Parus ater*); local resident
It breeds in widely separated localities at the lough. It is commonest in the woods at the west.

Sight records were rare following the severe winter of 1962/3, but they seem to have recovered since then.

LONG-TAILED TIT (*Aegithalos caudatus*); local resident
This, the least common of the tit family in Ireland, is well represented at the lake. Breeding was proved on 2 June 1975, but possibly also previous to this.

Small feeding parties are regularly encountered, especially in the copses on the Derry shore.

The hard winter 1962/3 had a temporary detrimental effect on the status of this bird at the lough.

TREE CREEPER (*Certhia familiaris*); local resident
Although breeding has not been conclusively proven it

Great Tit

doubtless occurs in the woods at the north western boundary of the lake.

It is occasionally seen amongst small parties of tits, foraging for insects on the fringes of the woods, outside the breeding season.

WREN (*Troglodytes troglodytes*); resident
The wren breeds throughout the area, often near human habitation. Observation of the population following the winter of 1962/3, indicated that this tiny bird is probably quite resilient to extreme cold.

DIPPER (*Cinclus cinclus*)
It is unlikely that this species breeds in the area as the habitat is not entirely suitable. The dipper has, however, been seen on a number of occasions, mostly in the canal at Toome, but also on the Bann itself, between Lough Neagh and Lough Beg.

MISTLE THRUSH (*Turdus viscivorus*); resident
A few pairs breed in the deciduous woods. In the winter, small parties mix with other thrushes but are the least abundant of the family.

FIELDFARE (*Turdus pilaris*); abundant winter visitor and passage migrant
Large gatherings, mixed with redwings, accumulate in the arable land near the lough. Arriving in mid-October, numbers generally reach a maximum in January and February. They dwindle steadily through March and the last ones have gone by mid-April.

In January 1976, a large build up occurred. By the end of the month there were a thousand mixed fieldfares and redwings, mostly in the area of the Creagh. On 12 February a single flock of 1,000 fieldfares was at the sandpits, with probably as many again in the rest of the area of Lough Beg. By 7 April only twelve remained.

This species appears to be more hardy than the red-wing in cold weather.

SONG THRUSH (*Turdus philomelos*); resident, breeding abundantly
Fair numbers are present in winter, associating with redwing and fieldfare. The resident stock is swollen by immigrants, probably largely from northern Britain.

Numbers are invariably less than the other northern European thrushes.

REDWING (*Turdus iliacus*); winter visitor and passage migrant
The flocks of this northern thrush are invariably smaller than those of the fieldfare, though 100 to 200 together in the later part of the winter is not uncommon. Many gather in the fields and hedgerows of the Creagh towards the end of the winter.

Following the hard winter of 1962/3, only small numbers were to be found around Lough Beg, indicating its apparent vulnerability to extreme cold.

BLACKBIRD (*Turdus merula*)
Resident, breeding abundantly throughout the area. Large numbers are present in the winter, due to winter immigration.

WHEATEAR (*Oenanthe oenanthe*); passage migrant in small numbers
It is more regular in the autumn than in the spring. The largest number in a day was nine on 18 September 1960.

Although they may be seen in the sandpits on passage, wheatears are most likely to be encountered in the boulder-strewn areas of the callow lands in the west.

Some of the migrants may be of the race *Oenanthe oenanthe leucorrhoa*, the Greenland race, as large, bulky individuals have been noticed on occasions.

Dipper

STONECHAT (*Saxicola torquata*); increasing: may
   breed in the area
Previously scarce inland: it had been recorded only as
an uncommon visitor to Lough Beg until the 1970s.
Pairs were seen on 31 May 1959 and 18 February 1962.
   It has been seen holding territory in the past few

years. The many recent sightings indicate that this
species may establish itself at the lake.

REDSTART (*Phoenicurus phoenicurus*); vagrant
A juvenile bird was observed on 11 August 1957, in
the woods bordering the Derry shore of the lough. It

Song Thrush opening a Snail

was considered that this bird may have been bred in the area.

ROBIN (*Erithacus rubecula*); resident
The robin breeds throughout the area, mainly in the proximity of buildings. A population study would un-doubtedly reveal a high density.

GRASSHOPPER WARBLER (*Locustella naevia*); local summer visitor
A few breeding pairs are to be found in less disturbed marshy locations, mostly in the south of the lough.

Wheatear

GD'A

The population appears to fluctuate from year to year.

SEDGE WARBLER (*Acrocephalus schoenobaenus*);
    summer visitor
This warbler is to be found near water, especially in reedy habitat, on both shores of the lough. It is most common in the sandpits at the south end where at least ten pairs have bred. However, since the development of some of this area, less are to be found there.

First arrivals are in late April and by May they are widespread. Autumn migrants have been found in the farm copses, well away from the lough shore.

Swallow

Gordon D'Arcy

71

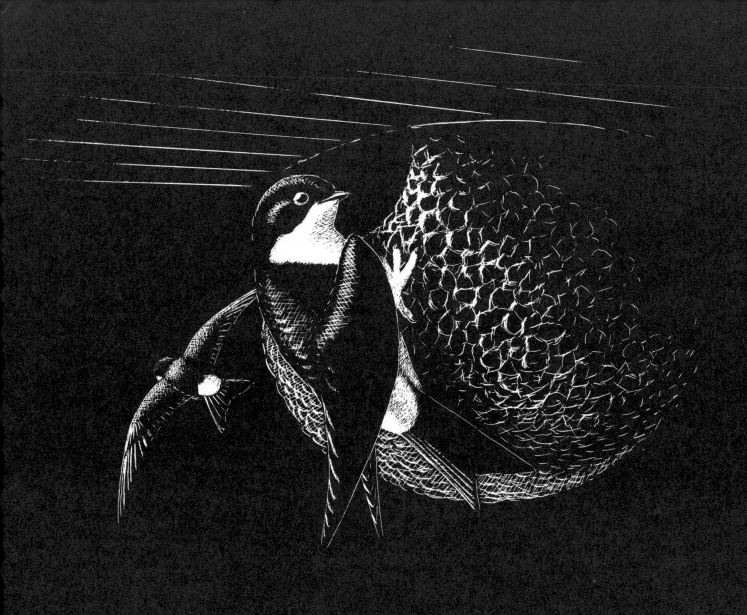

House Martin at nest

Gordon D'Arcy

72

Hooded Crows robbing Lapwings' nest

Gordon D'Arcy

73

Long-tailed Tits

Gordon D'Arcy

Sedge Warbler

BLACKCAP (*Sylvia atricapilla*); rare autumn migrant
This species has been trapped on a few occasions in the farmland on the western shore of the lough in recent years.

Intensive coverage of the woodland habitat in the summer months has yet to reveal singing birds which could be breeding in the area.

WHITETHROAT (*Sylvia communis*); local summer visitor

A few pairs breed in the thick undergrowth, mostly at the south end of the lough. It probably breeds locally on the Antrim shore of the lough, in suitable habitat. There has been a decline in recent years, reflecting a general pattern in the British Isles.

WILLOW WARBLER (*Phylloscopus trochilus*); summer visitor

Quite a few pairs breed in the area. Early arrivals appear in late March, the majority, however, reaching the lough in April. In the latter month, considerable numbers are to be heard singing in the trees and bushes on both the Antrim and the Derry shores.

A build-up of warblers takes place in the late summer. Composed mainly of this species, hundreds may be found along the Derry shore, especially on Church Island, and at the farm copses. This concentration probably represents pre-departure gathering, rather than passage migration.

CHIFFCHAFF (*Phylloscopus collybita*); summer visitor

Small numbers breed in the woods on both shores of the lough. The first arrivals are in late March, the species being well established by mid-April.

As it favours the trees rather than the more extensive scrub, the chiffchaff is less abundant than the willow warbler around the lough.

GOLDCREST (*Regulus regulus*); resident and winter visitor

This tiny bird is known to breed in a few of the wooded areas around the lough. Small flocks may be encountered in the autumn and winter. The exceptional number of about fifty was seen on 16 November 1959.

SPOTTED FLYCATCHER (*Muscicapa striata*); local summer visitor

A few pairs are found in the wooded areas on both sides of the lough. Family groups have been seen after the breeding season in the woods of the Ballyscullion Demesne and in the vicinity of Toome.

DUNNOCK (*Prunella modularis*); resident

The dunnock breeds abundantly throughout the area and next to the wren is the commonest small bird of the undergrowth.

MEADOW PIPIT (*Anthus pratensis*); resident and passage migrant

The meadow pipit breeds abundantly on both shores at Lough Beg.

A considerable migration takes place through the lough in the autumn, often associated with wagtails. Numbers of up to fifty or sixty are normal, but over a hundred may be present, as on 17 September 1975. It is difficult to assess whether this movement is of local pipits or of northern birds moving south via the Bann valley.

PIED WAGTAIL (*Motacilla alba*); passage migrant and resident

This species passes through Lough Beg in good numbers in the autumn, and in smaller numbers in the spring. As many as sixty have been seen in a day. They are to be found mainly in the open meadows, often associating with meadow pipits, in late August or September. An obvious 'fall' of this species was noted on 23 September 1976, when about 100 were seen.

Only a few pairs nest in the area, and it is unusual to see more than a few on a winter's day.

The sub-species *Motacilla alba alba*, known as the white wagtail, is a migrant mainly in the spring, in numbers of up to sixty. Passage in the autumn is much less pronounced.

Starlings going to roost

GREY WAGTAIL (*Motacilla cinerea*); local resident
Breeding occurs in the Ballyscullion Demesne, and perhaps also in one or two of the streams which flow into the lough at the western side. It is also believed to nest on the Antrim shore.

YELLOW WAGTAIL (*Motacilla flava*); rare visitor; previously bred
Up until summer 1942, or perhaps 1944 (see *Atlas of Breeding Birds of Great Britain and Ireland*), this species bred in the area in gradually decreasing numbers, until it finally vanished. This was probably the last remaining colony of yellow wagtail in Ireland.

A pair of the race *flavissima* was observed and suspected of breeding in the summer of 1968.

WAXWING (*Bombycilla garrulus*); irregular winter visitor in small numbers

Small parties have turned up, mostly at Toome, on a number of winters. Invariably small, flocks are generally less than twelve in number.

STARLING (*Sternus vulgaris*); resident and probable winter visitor
Breeds in most suitable locations: farms, occupied and derelict, dead trees, walls etc.

After the breeding season, flocking takes place. The local population is swollen in the winter by immigrants from other areas, possibly northern Europe.

GREENFINCH (*Carduelis chloris*); resident
Small numbers breed in the area.

Wintering flocks containing numbers of up to 200 may be seen in the open fields to the south and west of the lough. This species mixes with linnets, sparrows and other finches in these feeding flocks.

GOLDFINCH (*Carduelis carduelis*); occasional visitor to suitable habitat around the lake
Breeding occurs at Toome.

Small parties of up to a dozen birds make nomadic feeding visits to the rough ground, especially at the sandpits. Flocks are most likely to be encountered outside the breeding season.

SISKIN (*Carduelis spinus*); regular winter visitor in small numbers
Small parties turn up, feeding mainly on the alder cones in the wooded areas. The maximum number to come to my notice was a flock of twenty on 26 November 1975.

It has been suspected of breeding near the area, but this has yet to be substantiated.

LINNET (*Acanthis cannabina*); local resident
Breeding was first proven in August 1963, when an adult was seen feeding young. Suitable breeding habitat exists around the lake. About six pairs are known to nest at present at a locality on the eastern shore.

In the autumn and winter, linnets gather in dense feeding flocks in the open fields. These flocks may contain up to 200 individuals.

REDPOLL (*Acanthis flammea*)
It is to be found on both sides of the lough in the breeding season, though the localities are few. Small numbers visit the area outside the summer, and associate with other finches in the hedgerows. One of a northern sub-species was seen on 5 April 1964.

A mealy redpoll, *acanthis flammea flammea*, was seen near Toome on 16 October 1963. It was in the company of other redpolls and a variety of finches.

BULLFINCH (*Pyrrhula pyrrhula*); local resident; a few pairs breeding

The farms on the western side of the lough harbour most of the bullfinches in the area. They are also found in one or two localities on the Antrim shore. It is unusual to see more than half a dozen together.

CROSSBILL (*Loxia curvirostra*); vagrant
An adult male and a juvenile were seen on 12 August 1963.

CHAFFINCH (*Fringilla coelebs*); resident and winter visitor
Many pairs breed in the copses and woods throughout the area.

In the autumn, post-breeding flocks gather and take to the fields and hedgerows. Largest numbers, sometimes hundreds, are to be found in the winter, mostly in the area of the Creagh and are, at least in part, comprised of brightly coloured individuals of continental origin.

BRAMBLING (*Fringilla montifringilla*); rarity to the area
One record: a group of seven birds was seen at Toome on 17 January 1958.

On its irregular winter influxes to Northern Ireland, this species tends to appear mainly in coastal regions.

YELLOWHAMMER (*Emberiza citrinella*); resident
A local breeder, the yellowhammer shows an affinity for the areas of gorse. It is found chiefly along the Antrim shore, but also at the sandpits.

In winter, it can be found in small numbers amongst wandering parties of other finches.

REED BUNTING (*Emberiza schoeniclus*); resident
Many pairs breed in the marshy and reedy areas, especially in the sandpits. They take to the hedgerows and fields in winter, often associating with other finches in flocks.

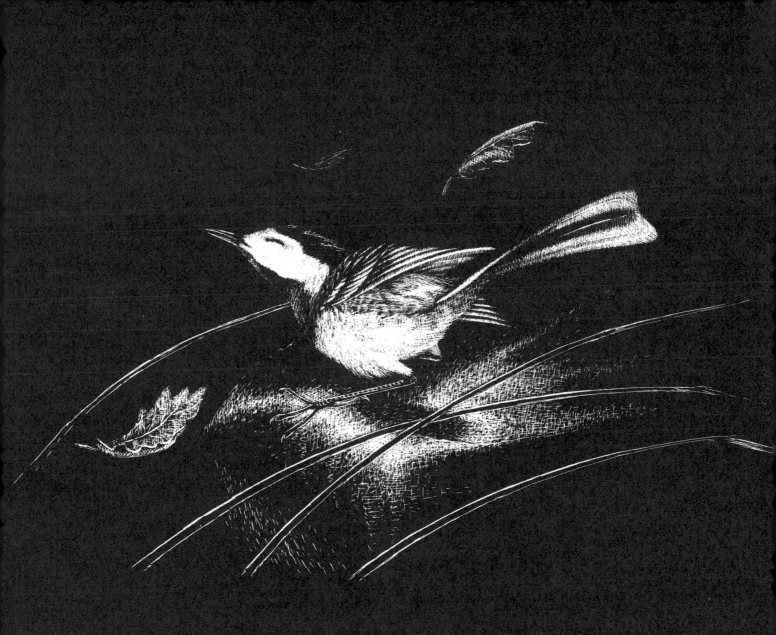

Pied Wagtail

Gordon D'Arcy

Snow Buntings

Gordon D'Arcy

House Sparrow with nest material

On 15 March 1964, twenty-seven were seen in one day.

SNOW BUNTING (*Plectrophenax nivalis*); uncommon winter visitor

Isolated stragglers turn up occasionally at the lake. On 15 December 1963, however, nine were seen.

HOUSE SPARROW (*Passer domesticus*); resident

A very common species, found chiefly around the farms in the breeding season.

Flocks gather in the fields and roads around the lough during the winter.

TREE SPARROW (*Passer montanus*); rare breeder

A pair with four juveniles was seen in willow trees near a ruin at the south end of the lough on 6 June 1964. Although not proven, breeding is considered a strong possibility at the locality. They were not found in subsequent years at the same locality. There are several nesting sites of this species around Lough Neagh: it may possibly extend its range to include more of the suitable habitat at Lough Beg.

———————

Appendix

ESCAPES AND OCCASIONAL VISITORS TO NEIGHBOURING LOUGH NEAGH

With some of the species which have been seen at Lough Beg, the possibility of escape from captivity (zoos, wildfowl collections, etc) cannot be ruled out. Where the possibility has existed, it has been mentioned in the systematic list. There is always an element of doubt where some of the wildfowl are concerned, as even the commonest species, like mallard, may be hand reared in artificial conditions.

An egyptian goose (*Alopochen aegyptiacus*) was shot at Toome in 1892, and was considered by C. D. Deane in his *Birds of Northern Ireland* to be a likely escape from captivity.

A flamingo (*Phoenicopterus species*) was seen on the lough during one of the NIOC wildfowl counts on 20 August 1967. It was identified by T. Ennis as a Chilean flamingo, and therefore an undoubted escape.

A substantial number of bird species has occurred on Lough Neagh which have not been recorded at Lough Beg. I believe that with continued intense observation, some of these will turn up at Lough Beg to augment the already impressive list.

Black throated diver (*Gavia arctica*); Slavonian grebe (*Podiceps auritus*); Manx shearwater (*Puffinus puffinus*); Bittern (*Botaurus stellaris*); Ring-necked duck (*Aythya collaris*); Ferruginous duck (*Aythya nycora*); Kentish plover (*Charadrius alexandrinus*); Red-necked phalarope (*Phalaropus lobatus*); Great skua (*Stercorarius skua*); Long-tailed skua (*Stercorarius longicaudus*); Auk species (*Alcidae*); Whinchat (*Saxicola rubetra*); Richard's pipit (*Anthus novaeseelandiae*); are among those birds recorded at the larger lake, and which have yet to turn up at Lough Beg.

THE ORNITHOLOGICAL YEAR AT LOUGH BEG
November-end January

Throughout the winter months the lough experiences repeated partial or total flooding.

The wintering wildfowl populations are established. There are some 500 swans (mostly whoopers) in the area. The flooded meadows harbour 2,500-4,000 surface feeding ducks, mainly wigeon and teal.

Diving ducks occur in variable numbers, but usually in thousands. Severe weather conditions drive large numbers of pochard and tufted duck west of their normal European wintering grounds. Masses of these birds pour into the Lough Neagh basin during these conditions. Up to 8,000 pochard have arrived at Lough Beg, only to be driven out to the larger lake by shooting. Hard-weather species like goosander, smew, red-crested pochard and long-tailed duck are most likely to turn up in this period.

Large concentrations of golden plover and lapwing, and to a lesser extent of dunlin and snipe, inhabit the open water meadows. A few jack snipe hide in the less disturbed areas. Isolated ruffs, redshank, greenshank, black-tailed godwit and other waders may remain behind throughout the winter.

In the surrounding woods and open ground, parties of fieldfares, redwings, linnets, redpolls and siskins are to be found. The brightly coloured continental chaffinch is abundant. Casual visitors include snow buntings, northern redpolls, waxwings and bramb-

Surface-feeding Ducks and Godwits

lings. Amongst the predators, the short-eared owl is regular and the peregrine is making increasingly regular visits.

February-early April

Certain species build up to large pre-migratory flocks.

Shoveler accumulate to 400 or 500, followed a little later by pintail, which may exceed 500 and on one occasion have nearly reached 1,000. Teal may exceed 2,000.

Amongst the diving ducks, goldeneye is perhaps the most note-worthy. They reach a peak of 300-450 and may be accompanied by small numbers of scaup. Small numbers of geese are seen in this period.

Hordes of wading birds gather at the lough in preparation for the mass exodus. Golden plover and lapwing comprise an accumulation of at least 5,000 birds in the western callow land. One of the most interesting waders of the interval is the black-tailed godwit. Arriving as an early migrant in February, it builds up to 300-500 by late March or early April.

Congregations of departing larks, thrushes, finches and up to 2,000 fieldfares have been noted in the open ground at the south end of the lough at this time.

Rarities include red-throated diver and raven.

Herons occupy their colony in the woods at the Ballyscullion Estate. Usually between a dozen and thirty breed and there is recent evidence that they may be expanding their range at the lough.

April-early June

Spring migration is in full swing.

Significant numbers of shoveler, pintail, teal and shelduck pass through, accompanied by small numbers of gadwall and the occasional garganey. Late migratory parties of geese and wild swans are also to be expected. Small numbers of goldeneye, pochard and scaup continue to move out via Lough Beg.

Black-tailed godwit, which have reached a peak at the beginning of April, tail off gradually, giving way to lesser numbers of whimbrel. They reach a peak at around the end of April and continue to move through, well into May.

Parties of ringed plover, golden plover, dunlin and redshank are to be seen, accompanied by the occasional grey plover, little stint, knot, turnstone, sanderling or bar-tailed godwit. More rarely, especially in May, the odd green or wood sandpiper, summer plumage ruff and spotted redshank, or little gull may appear on passage.

This is a marvellous period for the unexpected. Rarities which have been recorded are white stork, osprey, broad-billed sandpiper and lesser yellowlegs.

Summer visitors like martins, swallows, warblers, cuckoos and corncrakes reach Lough Beg early in this period, whilst wagtails, pipits and a trickle of wheatears pass through.

June-early August

It is convenient to use this period to discuss the breeding species of the area, although many will have nested before June.

Amongst the waterfowl, mallard, tufted duck and shelduck breed abundantly. A number of teal and shoveler and a few mergansers also nest. Pintail have bred occasionally, and pochard have nested once. Many pairs of coot, waterhen and mute swans rear their young on the lough, and a few pairs of great-crested grebes breed on the islands and in the reed beds.

There are four island colonies of black-headed gulls, amounting to some 700 pairs, accompanied on one of these by a few pairs of common terns.

Lapwing, redshank, snipe and curlew breed in fair numbers, whilst oystercatcher, dunlin, ringed plover and common sandpiper have only a rather tenuous hold as nesting species.

Golden Plover

GD'A

A pair of Goldeneye

Large populations of passerines are found in the woods and scrubland. Yellow wagtail, jay and possibly tree sparrow and partridge are no longer found, and others are represented by only a few pairs. Amongst the birds of prey, kestrel, sparrow hawk and long-eared own are known to breed annually, barn own having bred in the past.

August-end October

Post-breeding build-up occurs at the end of this interval, followed by eventual departure, and the arrival of passage migrants.

Mallard accumulate to a mass of between 2,000 and 3,500 in August, indicating the large numbers which breed in the northern part of the Lough Neagh basin. These are accompanied by a build-up of some 500 shoveler. In recent years, coot have begun to flock together in early autumn. Passage migrants swell the flock to a large congregation which may contain as many as 2,000 individuals by the latter part of the autumn.

Amongst the waders, common sandpipers have reached a peak and moved on by August. The main passage waders are ruffs, greenshanks, dunlins, knots, spotted redshank and redshank. Black-tailed godwit, whimbrel, ringed plover, grey plover, turnstone, with a variety of others, occur in lesser numbers.

Exciting rarities like Wilson's phalarope, Baird's sandpiper and goshawk have turned up in this season, whilst others like pectoral, buff-breasted and wood sandpipers are fairly regular.

Wader passage is heaviest in September, and fairly regular accompanying species are black terns, garganey, odd harriers and merlins, and a thin but regular passage of wheatears.

Swallows and swifts gather, often in thousands, and departing warblers are found in profusion in the wooded areas.

With the advent of October, pintail and shoveler show an influx, the first wild swans arrive from their Arctic breeding grounds, and occasional parties of geese fly through to the south. Golden plovers arrive in force, the majority, however, passing on through initially. It is at this time that the odd dowitcher or buff-breasted sandpiper has been seen in company with the plover flocks.

Towards the end of this period the numbers of the wintering species stabilise. Shooting causes considerable disturbance to the bird life and this, combined with the regular flooding, causes large variations in the avian population of Lough Beg in the winter months.

LOCAL NAMES OF SOME OF THE BIRDS

Some of the commoner species at Lough Beg are known to the people of the area by names not to be found in ornithological texts. I feel that these are worth recording in this book, as many are descriptive and endearing, and have been used by farmers, wildfowlers and local people for generations.

Great crested grebe	
(Summer plumage)	Tossle head
(Winter plumage)	Mal-rookam
Little grebe	Tam pudding
Heron	Heron-cran
Mallard	Wild duck
Wigeon	Baldy
Shoveler	Spoonbill
Tufted duck	Black wigeon
Pochard	Redhead
Goldeneye	Whistler
Red-breasted merganser	Sawbill
Whooper swan	Wedgehead
Coot	Slob
Oystercatcher	Sea magpie
Lapwing	Pee weet
Snipe	Meadow bleat
Redshank	Bleerie
Common tern	Sea swallow
Hooded crow	Grey crow
Blue tit	Billy blue bonnet
Wren	Chitty ran
Mistle thrush	Scraker
Fieldfare	Felt thrush
Meadow pipit	Moss cheeper
Greenfinch	Green linnet
Linnet	The grey
Redpoll	The rosy grey
Chaffinch	White-winged sparrow
Yellowhammer	Yellow yornie

Bibliography

Deane, C. D., *Birds of Northern Ireland* (1954).

Donaldson, J., 'Winter and passage wildfowl at Lough Beg', *Irish Naturalists' Journal* (1968).

Gouders, John, *Where to watch birds in Europe* (1970).

Ruttledge, Scoope and Kennedy, *Birds of Ireland*.

Ruttledge, R. F., *Ireland's birds* (1966).

Sharrock, J. T. R., *The atlas of breeding birds in Britain and Ireland* (1976).

Sharrock, J. T. R., *The birds of Cape Clear* (1969).

Tree, A. J., *Lough Beg bulletin* (Ulster Society for the Protection of Birds) (1959).

Ussher and Warren, *Birds of Ireland* (1900).

Watson, P. S. and Donaldson, J., *Lough Beg report* (1963).

NIOC, *Lough Neagh basin wildfowl counts* (1965-1969).

IWC, *Irish bird reports* (1953-1975).

Department of Lands, *The Wexford wildfowl reserve* (1969).

Proceedings of the Belfast Naturalists' Field Club (1889-1900).

Index

Page numbers in italics denote illustrations.

Latin Index

Index to Latin names of bird species in the list

Acanthis cannabina, 78
  flammea, 78
Accipiter
  gentilis, 37
  nisus, 37
Acrocephalus
  schoenobaenus. 70
Aegithalos caudatus, 65
Alauda arvensis, 60
Alcedo atthis, 60
Anas acuta, 26
  clypeata, 26
  crecca, 24
  crecca carolinensis, 25
  discors, 26
  penelope, 26
  platyrhynchos, 24
  querquedula, 26
  strepera, 26
Anser albifrons flavirostris,
  31
  anser, 31
  brachyrhynchus, 31
Anthus
  pratensis, 76
Apus
  apus, 58
Ardea cinerea, 24
Arenaria interpres, 42
Asio
  flammeus, 58
  otus, 58
Aythya
  ferina, 29
  fuligula, 29
  marila, 29

Bombycilla garrulus, 77
Branta
  leucopsis, 31
Bucephala
  clangula, 29

Calidris
  alba, 54

alpina, 52
bairdii, 54
canutus, 51
ferruginea, 52
fuscicollis, 52
melanotos, 52
minuta, 52
Caprimulgus
  europaeus, 58
Carduelis carduelis, 78
  chloris, 77
  spinus, 78
Certhia
  familiaris, 65
Charadrius
  hiaticula, 42
Chlidonias
  niger, 56
Ciconia ciconia, 24
Cinclus cinclus, 67
Circus
  cyaneus, 37
Clangula hyemalis, 30
Columba
  oenas, 56
  palumbus, 58
Corvus corax, 60
  corone cornix, 65
  corone corone, 65
  frugilegus, 65
  monedula, 65
Crex crex, 40
Cuculus canorus, 58
Cygnus bewickii, 37
  cygnus, 31
  olor, 31

Delichon urbica, 60
Dendrocopos
  major, 60

Egretta
  garzetta, 24
Emberiza

citrinella, 78
  schoeniclus, 78
Erithacus rubecula, 69

Falco
  columbarius, 38
  peregrinus, 38
  tinnunculus, 38
Fringilla coelebs, 78
  montifringilla, 78
Fulica atra, 40
Fulmarus glacialis, 23

Gallinula chloropus, 40
Garrulus glandarius, 65
Gavia
  immer, 23
  stellata, 23
Grus grus, 39

Haematropus
  ostralegus, 40
Hirundo
  rustica, 60

Larus argentatus, 54
  canus, 55
  fuscus graellsii, 54
  glaucoides, 56
  hyperboreus, 55
  marinus, 54
  minutus, 56
  ridibundus, 56
Limicola falcinellus, 54
Limnodromus
  scolopaceus/griseus, 43
Limosa lapponica, 44
  limosa, 44
Locustella
  naevia, 69
Loxia curvirostra, 78
Lymnocryptes minimus, 43

Melanitta
  nigra, 30
Mergus albellus, 30
  merganser, 30
  serrator, 30
Motacilla alba, 76
  cinerea, 77
  flava, 77
Muscicapa
  striata, 76

Netta rufina, 29
Numenius arquata, 44
  phaeopus, 44

Oceanodroma
  Leucorrhoa, 23
Oenanthe
  oenanthe, 67

Pandion haliaetus, 37
Parus ater, 65
  caeruleus, 65
  major, 65
Passer domesticus
  montanus, 82
Perdix perdix, 38
Phalacrocorax
  aristotelis, 24
  carbo, 24
Phalaropus fulicarius, 54
  tricolor, 54
Phasianus colchicus, 39
Philomachus pugnax, 54
Phoenicurus
  phoenicurus, 68
Phylloscopus
  collybita, 76
  trochilus, 76
Pica pica, 65
Platalea leucorodia, 24
Plectrophenax nivalis, 82
Pluvialis apricaria, 42
  squatarola, 42